Strange Tales
about Jesus

D1453154

Strange Tales about Jesus

A Survey of Unfamiliar Gospels

Per Beskow

FORTRESS PRESS   PHILADELPHIA

Translated from the Swedish, *Fynd och fusk i Bibelns värld*, copyright ©
1979 Per Beskow, Lund, and Proprius förlag, Stockholm.

English translation © 1983 by Per Beskow

First Fortress Press Edition 1983

Library of Congress Cataloging in Publication Data

Beskow, Per, 1926–
    Strange tales about Jesus.

    Rev. translation of: Fynd och fusk i Bibelns värld.
    Includes bibliographical references.
    1. Apocryphal books (New Testament) — Criticism,
interpretation, etc. 2. Jesus Christ — Biography —
Apocryphal and legendary literature. I. Title.
BS2840.B47 1983   229'.8   82–16001
ISBN 0-8006-1686-3

9752K82   Printed in the United States of America   1–1686

Contents

Preface to
the American Edition

Are there perhaps unknown or disregarded Gospels which would give us an entirely different picture of Jesus than the conventional one? Books and notices in the press sometimes tell us about secret documents that would cast a new light on Jesus, but have been suppressed by the churches or the clergy. It is often said that these documents are hidden in some archives, waiting to be published and made known to the world. Such reports, however, are often met with disbelief by established biblical research, which is said to be controlled by the clergy in order to serve the aims of Christian apologetics.

On the part of the scholars, this kind of literature is usually surrounded by a wall of silence. It is virtually unknown to most exegetes so that when an alleged Gospel manuscript is published, it remains generally ignored without being reviewed. In fact, it is considered poor manners to write about these books, at least without an apology to the reader. This, I think, is an unwise attitude. The alleged Gospels constitute a literary genre in their own right which has existed almost as long as Christianity. Such "Gospels" have a popular character and are read by ordinary people who do not care for more serious scholarly works.

As a young student exploring the bookshelves of the theological faculty library in Uppsala, I came upon Edgar J. Goodspeed's *Strange New Gospels*[1] and was amazed at the great number of modern apocrypha, legends, and forgeries about Jesus that he discussed. I found this book to be a refreshing change from the heavy German Bible commentaries that we were supposed to read, but I certainly did not have the slightest thought that I might one day try to pursue Goodspeed's work. Only many years later, in 1976, did I get the idea of holding a radio talk on "modern Jesus legends," which gave rise to so much interest that I decided to write a book on this subject.

It is certainly not my ambition to replace Goodspeed's excellent work, which is still indispensable for anyone seeking information about alleged books of the Bible. But considerable time has passed, and more apocryphal books have appeared. Also, the revised edition of Goodspeed's book, *Modern Apocrypha,* has been out of print for a long while.

As I understand it, then, there is still need for a survey like Goodspeed's especially at a time when so many new religious movements have appeared, sometimes presenting documents of a doubtful antiquity. My choice of apocrypha has perhaps been made from a European point of view. But most of the apocrypha included in this book are still available in print, and may puzzle some who read them. Moreover, in a number of instances I have tried to clear up a few mysteries that Goodspeed left unsolved.

This book was first written for a Swedish public and included a great number of Swedish bibliographic references. I have now translated the book into English and have rewritten those passages which I consider of less interest to American readers. For the same reason I have also omitted two entire chapters of the original Swedish edition. On the other hand, some additional matter has been inserted in the English edition. I am conscious of my lack of firsthand knowledge of American books on modern apocryphal works, and I have therefore had to rely occasionally on Goodspeed for information about these books. Since most of the apocrypha, however, originated in Europe, it has been easier for me than it was for Goodspeed to trace their beginnings.

1

The Dream of the Marvelous Book Discovery

As long as human beings have been able to read and write, we have been fascinated by the possibility of making the sensational discovery of an unknown text. In Egyptian, Greek, and Roman literature from antiquity, there is a wealth of stories about books or letters which have fallen down from heaven or which have been found in tombs, temples, or ancient libraries, and which contain revelations, oracles, or magical recipes. The Austrian scholar Wolfgang Speyer has written a book on this theme, which is a veritable gold mine for the interested reader.[2] It certainly happened in antiquity, as in our own time, that valuable manuscripts could be discovered on happy occasions. The finding of a law book—possibly Deuteronomy—in the temple of Jerusalem during the reign of King Josiah (2 Kings 22:8–13) may be such an authentic book find. These cases of real discoveries, however, are totally submerged by the flood of forgeries, legends, and romantic tales.

Already in antiquity there was a rich variation between fantastic and realistic stories about book discoveries. The fantastic story has its place in religious literature of a more popular kind and in fiction in general, where book finds are a standard topic. The realistic story, on the other hand, is rather artful and has a concrete aim. It is this latter kind that deserves the name of forgery, and even today it is possible to make a certain distinction between fraud and fiction. But as we shall see in the following, it is often difficult to maintain this distinction in practice.

Early Christian literature also has examples of alleged book finds. During the early postapostolic times, a popular and legendary literature flourished which we used to designate as "New Testament apocrypha."[3] These were alleged Gospels, acts of the apostles, and letters or apocalypses written by apostles. They all belong to a time

1

later than that of the New Testament writings, and the early church was well aware of this fact when the New Testament was gathered into a canon. Some of these apocrypha were rejected as heretical; but others, which did not contradict the faith of the church, were allowed to live on, although on a lower level as legendary-but-tolerated folk literature. Very popular were the so-called infancy Gospels, which embroidered the brief accounts in the New Testament Gospels about the childhood and youth of Jesus. Other apocrypha, which have retained their popularity until our own time, are *The Letter of Abgarus* and *The Letter of Lentulus.*[4]

New Testament apocrypha are usually written in the name of an apostle, such as *The Gospel of Peter* or *The Apocalypse of Paul.* There is a story about the discovery of *The Apocalypse of Paul* — a story of the kind that will later be familiar to us. Several versions of this story exist, but the Greek version runs as follows:

> In the consulate of Theodosius Augustus the Younger and of Cynegius, a certain respected man was living in Tarsus in the house which had once belonged to St. Paul; during the night an angel appeared to him and gave him a revelation telling him to break up the foundations of the house and to make public what he found. But he thought this was a delusion. However the angel came the third time and scourged him and compelled him to break up the foundations. And when he had dug, he discovered a marble box which was inscribed on the sides; in it was the revelation of St. Paul and the shoes in which he used to walk when he was teaching the word of God. But he was afraid to open the box and brought it to a judge; the judge accepted it and sent it as it was, sealed with lead, to the Emperor Theodosius; for he was afraid it might be something else. And when the emperor received it, he opened it and found the revelation of St. Paul. After a copy had been made, he sent the original manuscript to Jerusalem.[5]

Not even in antiquity was this story accepted without reservation. Sozomen, who wrote his *Church History* between A.D. 430 and 450, described the apocalypse as a forgery and added that none of the ancients had known it. According to Sozomen, this document dates from the time of the emperor mentioned in the legend. Sozomen's work is a good illustration of how early Christian authors could exhibit a critical mind before alleged documents and revelations. It goes without saying, then, that *The Apocalypse of Paul*

2

was not written by Saint Paul; its earliest parts may stem from the second century, but its final version is more likely from the end of the fourth century, just as Sozomen presumed.

The Apocalypse of Paul is an excellent example of the difficulty in drawing a clear line between legitimate or genuine pseudepigraphy and forgery. Biblical scholars have long been indulgent about this kind of authorship, and it is often said in textbooks that in antiquity it was allowed to write in others' names and to imitate religious or profane works without coming into conflict with current moral values. In later years it has been increasingly clear that the concept of forgery was by no means foreign to antiquity, and that the existence of pseudepigrapha was a problem also in the early church.[6]

The Middle Ages were well versed in the art of forgery, but it was ecclesiastical documents, letters of privilege, and the like that were the subject of this activity. Little was told about book finds, but a well-known interest in discoveries of tombs of saints and of relics together with pious local patriotism was a constant temptation to fraud. The "letters from heaven" are certainly of medieval origin; they seem to have originated in the sixth century and were spread in various versions until our own time. They are alleged letters from God or Christ and are said to have fallen down from heaven and to have been found in various places. *The Letter of Lentulus* with its description of the looks of Jesus also belongs to medieval literature.[7]

Then came the era of Renaissance humanism with its call for a return to the sources. The increasing interest in ancient documents aroused anew the dream of the book discovery. In the Gospel forgeries from this time, an important role was given to the circumstances of the alleged discovery. The *Gospel of Barnabas*, from an indeterminable time between the fourteenth and sixteenth centuries, was said to have been found by a monk in the library of Pope Sixtus V. *The Death Warrant of Jesus* was said to have been uncovered in Vienne (south of France) and in Aquila (middle Italy) respectively. Here we can also find elements from earlier legends of book discoveries such as the interest in the various boxes for the Aquila document, the same motif that we have already seen in the story about *The Apocalypse of Paul.*

But it is in the nineteenth century that the stories of book finds got into full swing, and under new conditions. It was at this time that a radical biblical criticism was first heard, and the reliability of the Gospel stories began to be questioned also in public debate. In addition, fiction demonstrated a fresh interest in Jesus; novel writers gave him new features, and he was seen as a sensitive and morally superior teacher rather than as the Son of God. The border between fiction and forgery could not always be kept clear.

The middle of the nineteenth century was a time of many real manuscript discoveries, such as Constantin Tischendorf's famous find of the *Codex Sinaiticus* at the Monastery of St. Catherine in the Sinai desert. The faked stories about book discoveries were now given a pseudo-scientific character, for there were more severe criteria used to decide about the authenticity of documents. Thus these book finds became proper frauds more than before. But the older literary genres lived on. Letters from heaven were copied throughout the nineteenth century. Moreover, the "find" of *The Book of Mormon* also belongs to a prescientific society, even if the awakening interest in Egyptology and in archaeology in general has given some support to Joseph Smith's work.

The stories about the discoveries now become more realistic than fantastic and aim to prove the authenticity of the document. *The Essene Letter* is said to have been found in the library of an Egyptian monastery; *The Report of Pilate*, in the Vatican library; and *The Archko Volume*, also in the Vatican library and in the library of Hagia Sophia in Istanbul. *The Death Warrant of Jesus* from the sixteenth century received a new form and became a copperplate, and would have been discovered by Dominique Vivant Denon during his legitimated robber expedition in the company of the Napoleonic troops.

The interest in India at the end of the nineteenth century gave fresh ideas to alleged book discoveries. Nicolas Notovitch "discovered" *The Life of Saint Issa* in 1887 during an adventurous journey in the western borderland of Tibet. At the same time, the Reverend G. J. R. Ouseley claimed to have gotten hold of a Tibetan manuscript on *The Gospel of the Holy Twelve*, but this time delivered by spiritist means. Levi H. Dowling's *Aquarian Gospel* also belongs to the same era, which becomes obvious in the passage where Jesus preaches the doctrine of reincarnation.

Quite unexpectedly the twentieth century has given us a number of real discoveries of manuscripts which are more important than any earlier finds. The Coptic-Gnostic library of Nag-Hammadi (1945), the Dead Sea Scrolls (1947), the Jewish fragments from Masada (1963–65), and, most lately, the sensational finds in the Monastery of St. Catherine (1975) have given scholars an immense amount of material for future work. But stories of alleged finds have followed in the traces of these real discoveries. The later parts of *The Gospel of Peace* (or *The Gospel of the Essenes*), for example, have obvious similarities to the Dead Sea Scrolls, and Donovan Joyce's *Jesus Scroll* is directly inspired by the Masada finds.[8] May we, perhaps, understand this as a kind of modern folklore, where the belief in revelations or in letters from heaven has been superseded by a kind of religious science fiction, where the credulity appears under the cloak of scholarly work? As we all know, it is possible to make people believe in the strangest things, as long as they are presented as "scientific discoveries."

A Swedish journalist with feminist leanings announced a couple of years ago that a new Gospel had been found, revealing that Jesus was a woman. The journalist in question is fairly well known as one who is fond of practical jokes, and nothing more has been heard about this Gospel either in Sweden or abroad. But the interesting point is how disturbed some people became about this story and about the possibility that it might be true. The idea of the unknown Jesus manuscript seems to lie deep in our unconscious, and many of us seem to hope or fear that such a manuscript might appear. At the same time, the manuscript might be filled with the most varied content according to the topic of the day. Everything seems to point to a future when new topics and new ideologies will be supported by legendary book discoveries, which we have not yet heard of.

2

The Reader in Face of the Document

This book is mainly about forgeries. Some readers may feel confused and disturbed by the amount of alleged biblical manuscripts, lost scrolls, and strange assertions about Jesus. Is it possible at all to know what is genuine and what is not in the case of Jesus?

First of all, the writings of our New Testament are certainly no forgeries. They are documents of faith. It is possible, of course, to reject these documents as they were rejected in their own time, but it cannot be denied that they stem from the earliest Christian time. Concerning other, more unfamiliar documents, however, it is not always possible to give a general answer. There are forgeries which are so unskillfully made that the general reader can immediately unmask the fraud, but there are also some documents that the specialists disagree about, such as *The Secret Gospel of Mark.* But in other cases the nonprofessional can probably decide about an alleged document, if he only learns to observe certain essential details.

Falsifying a biblical writing is not an easy task: it requires knowledge of the language as well as of ancient manuscripts. If *The Secret Gospel of Mark* is a writing from antiquity, as will be discussed later, then there are only four modern Bible forgeries that I know about which have been written in ancient languages. The first is *The Report of Pilate*, partly published in Latin in 1879. The second is an apocryphal infancy Gospel in Latin, written by the French poet Catulle Mendès, and published in 1904 probably just as entertainment or as a means to confuse scholars.[9] The third is a clumsy Greek parchment codex with a *Gospel of Josephus,* said to have been unearthed in Rome in 1927. Soon enough it transpired that it was the work of two Italians, Moccia and Gardella, made to advertise a book that Moccia was about to produce. The latest contribution is a Hebrew text of fifteen pages, said to be the text of some fragments of the *Gospel of Peace*, which Edmond Szekely claimed to have found in the library of Monte Cassino in the 1920s. These fragments seem instead to have been produced half a century later.

Most forgers have followed the easier path of publishing a "translation" from an original that is lost or hidden somewhere. Notovitch's *The Life of Saint Issa* is said to be in Himalaya, and Ouseley's *The Gospel of the Holy Twelve* is said to have been hidden in the Vatican by the clergy. The original of *The Essene Letter* supposedly can be borrowed from the Pythagorean or Masonic Society in Germany, which is said to have possessed it for about 150 years; but the difficult point is to find their address. All forgers are not as unscrupulous as Edmond Szekely: his Gospel is said to exist not only in the Hebrew fragments mentioned above, but also in two complete manuscripts, one in Vienna and one in Rome. The problem is that nobody else has ever seen them.

It is imperative that the editor of a manuscript be able to tell the reader where the manuscript is and how other scholars may be able to get hold of it. That is why the debate about *The Secret Gospel of Mark* is so heated, for it is only the editor, Morton Smith, who has seen the manuscript, and that was more than twenty years ago. But there are at least photographs of this manuscript, and that is far more than may be said about the majority of the alleged documents discussed in this book. As a rule, one should be skeptical about alleged discoveries of this kind, especially if they are said to have a sensational content. It is better to wait until more certain information is given concerning where they are to be found and who is in charge of them.

Not only are the circumstances of the find important, but so is the document itself. A close study of its style and content may often reveal as much as its external history. The revealing traits are not always found in the main content of the writing, but rather in small and seemingly unimportant details.

After the World War II bombings, the *Marienkirche* in Lübeck was restored, and the restorer found some remarkable Gothic wall paintings, which were honored by becoming the motif for a West German series of stamps. It later transpired that the paintings were pure forgeries, painted on the wall by Lothar Malskat, the restorer's assistant. Malskat had also been at work in other churches, and one of his "restorations" in Schleswig was revealed as such by a mistake that he made. In one place he put a turkey into the picture, yet there were no turkeys in Europe until after the discovery of America.

Such "turkeys" will be noted many times in the following. Often they are just anachronisms, names or things that belong to another period — usually a later one — than the alleged time of the document. In other cases they are geographic impossibilities or confusions of persons or places. Sometimes they are quotations from books written in later centuries, which clearly disclose the fraud.

It may be more difficult to detect stylistic mistakes, even if some of these may be quite evident, as in *The Essene Letter*. It is especially important that the reader not be impressed by the solemn "biblical language," which is quite common in our kind of literature, and which is often influenced by the King James Version. The division into chapters and verses also looks "biblical," but is no sign of authenticity. On the contrary, genuine documents are never divided in this way, unless the editor has been undiscriminating enough to make them. The divisions of our Bible are not older than the Middle Ages.

I would also like to mention some books that have not been included in this edition. The Swedish edition contains many references to Scandinavian editions, which have been left out here. Two entire chapters have also been omitted. One is a Life of Christ, spread by the Mazdaznan movement and written by the founder of this movement, Dr. Otoman Zar-Adusht Ha'nish (*alias* Otto Hanisch), in the early twentieth century. The second is a Swedish pseudo-Gospel for children, in which Jesus is described as a Marxist revolutionary. None of these books are likely to fall into the hands of the American reader.

Some of the books described by Goodspeed have not been mentioned here for the simple reason that I have never become familiar with them. For information about them the reader is referred to Goodspeed's still very useful work. They are *The 27th chapter of Acts*, *The Second Book of Acts*, *The Letter of Benan*, and *The Book of Jasher*.

There is another category, however, which for various reasons I have left out, namely those books which claim to have been transmitted by direct revelation, and for which no alleged book discovery is implied. Goodspeed mentions such a book entitled *Oahspe*, which was first published in 1882 and is still read in some circles. A more modern specimen of this literary genre is *The Urantia Book* published by the Urantia Society in Chicago. Both of these works are most extensive and contain a great deal of cosmology. *The Urantia Book* also has a "biblical" part about the youth of Jesus and his travels, with many similarities to books such as *The Aquarian Gospel*. Other books with claims of direct inspiration are published by the Aetherius Society in England, including a Gospel allegedly written by the Virgin Mary. In another example, an Irish woman, Miss Geraldine D. Cummins, received "messages" in 1923 and had them published in 1928 under the title *The Scripts of Cleophas;* the real author was said to be Jesus' disciple of that name who is mentioned in Luke 24.[10]

Books of this kind will defy any argument about their lack of authenticity. Like the prophecies of the Old Testament, they claim to be heavenly messages. How can you prove that they are not? It may be that some of the pretended communications are poorly written, or that they contain obvious references to what the communicator may have read in world literature. But in the first case, poor writing is a matter of taste; in the second case, we should not forget that even the Apocalypse of John contains reminiscences of earlier Jewish literature. We may admire or deplore these messages, but we cannot determine their authenticity by scholarly means.

We cannot draw a distinctive line between these inspired books and alleged book discoveries, for there is the peculiar phenomenon of a double provenance. Some books pretend to have been inspired from above and also to have been discovered by their "editors," who do not seem to understand what strange coincidences they want their readers to accept. For instance, *The Book of Mormon* was written on golden plates and hidden in the earth, or so it is said, yet it was revealed to Joseph Smith by an angel, and Smith's translation was made not from the plates directly but by looking into certain stones. The Reverend Ouseley read his *Gospel of the Holy Twelve* in nightly visions, but he claimed that it was also an Aramaic manuscript, brought to Rome by a Franciscan friar. *The Aquarian Gospel* is in the same category as the *Oahspe* or *The Urantia Book*, but it has often been mistaken as the text of an ancient manuscript, which is why it has been included here.

3

The Gospel According to the Koran

The borderline between ancient and modern apocrypha is somewhat vague. One may ask whether a Renaissance forgery such as *The Gospel of Barnabas* should be included in a book on modern apocrypha. But it is only in our own century that it has begun to play an important part in religious debate, and it has caused such interest in the Arab world of today, that it deserves to be the first item in our review of Jesus apocrypha.

The Gospel of Barnabas was discovered in the beginning of the eighteenth century by the Prussian councillor J. F. Cramer, who had acquired the only known Italian manuscript in Amsterdam. It has the following lengthy title: *True Gospel of Jesus, called Christ, a new prophet sent by God to the world: according to the description of Barnabas, his apostle.* In 1709, Cramer lent the manuscript to John Toland, a famous theologian in the Era of Enlightenment, who became the first to publish some extracts from the Gospel. It was not until 1907, however, that *The Gospel of Barnabas* was published in its entirety; an English translation was included. The editors were Canon Lonsdale Ragg, Anglican chaplain in Venice, and his sister Laura. The manuscript was then in the Imperial Library in Vienna, now known as the National Library, where it remains to this day.[11]

Even John Toland could see that the statements in the Gospel bore strange similarities to the teachings of Islam about Jesus. The introduction of a Spanish version of the book tells us how a friar named Fra Marino had found the Gospel in the library of Pope Sixtus V, at a moment when the Holy Father had taken a little nap. The friar is said to have been so impressed by the reading that he converted to Islam. This story undoubtedly lacks historical basis; it has a curious parallel in the Gospel itself, where Nicodemus finds

11

the original Book of Moses in the house of the high priest (Chapter 192).

The two British editors believed that *The Gospel of Barnabas* was written between the fourteenth and sixteenth centuries by a former Christian, probably an Italian, who had converted to Islam, and who wanted to produce a Gospel in accordance with the statements about Jesus in the Koran. There are some references to the year of jubilee instituted by Pope Boniface VIII in 1300 (Chapters 82–83), which sets a starting point for the present recension of the Gospel. The original intention was that a jubilee should be celebrated every hundredth year, which is also stated in *The Gospel of Barnabas*. In 1349, however, Pope Clement VI decided that the celebration should take place every fiftieth year; this might indicate that the Gospel was written in the first half of the fourteenth century.

Recent research, however, indicates a more ancient origin for parts of the Gospel. We find traces in it of an early Judeo-Christian tradition from Syria or Palestine, which is related to that of the so-called Pseudo-Clementines of early Christian times. This certainly increases the value of *The Gospel of Barnabas* as a source for our understanding of early Christianity and of early asceticism, but the Islamic traits certainly belong to the final recension.

When the English translation was published, many Muslims took an interest in the remarkable writing. Here was a Gospel which was in accordance with the Koran and therefore superior to the canonical Gospels. Mirza Ghulam Ahmad, the founder of the Ahmadiyya movement in India, of whom we shall hear more later, used *The Gospel of Barnabas* as early as 1899, eight years before its publication.[12] When the Oxford edition appeared in 1907, it was supported by those involved with the Cairo periodical *al-Manar*, which published the first edition in Arabic in 1908. Many new editions have followed, and *The Gospel of Barnabas* is still as important as ever in the Arab world and in the Islamic mission to the West. When I visited the Islamic Cultural Centre in London in 1979, I found an impressive stock of this Gospel in English, intended for free distribution.

A special trait of the Gospel is that Barnabas is described as one of the twelve disciples, and he — not Peter — is given the first place. He is also given the task of writing down the teachings of Jesus. This seems odd to the Bible reader, for no Barnabas is mentioned among the Twelve either in the New Testament or in the ancient apocrypha. The Apostle Barnabas of the New Testament was not one of the disciples of Jesus and did not come into the story until Acts 4:36, where he appears as a member of the primitive Christian Church in Jerusalem.

The teaching of *The Gospel of Barnabas* is expressed first in the prologue: ". . . many, being deceived of Satan, under pretence of piety, are preaching most impious doctrine, calling Jesus Son of God, repudiating the circumcision ordained of God forever, and permitting every unclean meat: among whom also Paul hath been deceived, whereof I speak not without grief." This is a striking beginning, for circumcision and food laws, which are important to Islam, are some of the rules that St. Paul wanted the Gentiles to be free from. The author also mentions the title of the Son of God, which a few exegetes of our own time have also wanted to assign to St. Paul. As the full title of the document indicates, *The Gospel of Barnabas* does not allow that Jesus should be the Messiah. Although he is "called" the Messiah, this title by rights belongs to Mohammed. As we shall see, Mohammed is also prophetically announced in the Gospel.

The central events of *The Gospel of Barnabas* are similar to those of the canonical Gospels. Gabriel comes to Mary with the Annunciation as in the Gospel of Luke, the Magi visit Jesus as in Matthew, and Joseph and Mary flee with the child to Egypt. But John the Baptist is missing in these first chapters, perhaps not without reason: Jesus has no forerunner, for he is himself the forerunner of the real Messiah, who is Mohammed.

The call of Jesus to his task also has obvious Islamic traits. Jesus and Mary are on the Mount of Olives when Gabriel appears surrounded by an infinite multitude of angels. He presents to Jesus "a shining mirror, a book, which descended into the heart of Jesus" (Chapter 10). At the call of Mohammed it was the same Angel Gabriel who appeared, and the descent of the shining book into Jesus corresponds to the Islamic belief that the heavenly Koran was sent down to us and received by Mohammed. It is also possible, however, that the author was influenced by medieval letters from heaven; we shall return to them in a following chapter.

Throughout the Gospel Jesus constantly denies any divine status in his teaching. There is also a sternness in his rebuking of the Pharisees with frequent curses, which seems strange to the Jesus that we know from the canonical Gospels.

The teaching of *The Gospel of Barnabas* appears with full evidence in the passage where Jesus tells his disciples about the Creation and the Fall. When Adam is created, he sees a writing in the air with the Islamic confession: "There is only one God, and Mohammed is the messenger of God" (Chapter 39). Jesus tells James (Chapter 43) that the Messiah descends not from Isaac, as the Jews believe, but from Ishmael, from whom the only true Messiah — Mohammed — will descend. Accordingly, it is not Isaac but Ishmael whom Abraham is ordered to sacrifice. Finally, Jesus declares that he has seen Mohammed in a vision and cries out: "O Mohammed, God be with thee, and may he make me worthy to untie thy shoelaces, for obtaining this I shall be a great prophet and holy one of God" (Chapter 44).

The passion story is also adjusted to suit the teaching of the Koran that Jesus never died on the cross but was taken up into heaven uninjured. Jesus returns from Gethsemane to his house, where the eleven disciples are asleep. Then the four archangels — Gabriel, Michael, Raphael and Uriel — enter by the south window and carry him to the third heaven (Chapter 215). Meanwhile, the soldiers, with Judas as their guide, draw near to the house in order to arrest Jesus. Here the face of Judas is changed so that all mistake him for Jesus, and in spite of his protests he is taken to Golgotha and is crucified (Chapters 216–17). The angels carry Jesus back to earth, and he appears to Mary and the disciples and declares that he will be with God until near the end of the world. But the men of the world will believe that he has died on the cross until the arrival of Mohammed, the messenger of God (Chapters 218–20).

This Muslim Gospel certainly shows what an important position Jesus occupies in Islam. He is sent by God; he may even be called the Word (*Logos*) of God; he has an important task in the divine economy; and he shall someday return at the judgment. Thus Jesus has a higher rank in Islam than he has for many who call themselves Christians today. But the Jesus of Islam is certainly not the Jesus of the New Testament. Islam especially rejects the doctrine of Jesus as the Son of God; since this is misunderstood as if God is his father in a crudely physical way, Islam accordingly rejects this as blasphemy. Islam and the New Testament also cannot be reconciled regarding the crucifixion of Jesus, which is expressly denied by the Koran. There is thus no place for a resurrection, yet the ascension of Jesus is affirmed. It all seems confusing and paradoxical to a Christian.

It is essential to understand the position of Jesus in Islam when we wish to bring Muslims and Christians closer together. But a meaningful dialogue will require, among many other things, an insight from the Muslim side that *The Gospel of Barnabas* is not an original Christian source, and that it will never have a chance of being accepted by Christians.

4

The Copperplate from Aquila

Sentence rendered by Pontius Pilate, acting governor of lower Galilee, stating that Jesus of Nazareth shall suffer death on the cross. In the seventeenth year of the reign of the Emperor Tiberius and on the twenty-seventh [or twenty-fifth] day of March, in the most holy city of Jerusalem, during the pontificate of Annas and Caiaphas, Pontius Pilate, governor of lower Galilee, sitting in the presidential chair of the praetory, condemns Jesus of Nazareth to die on the cross between [two] thieves, the great and notorious evidence of the people saying:

1. Jesus is a seducer.
2. He is seditious.
3. He is the enemy of the Law.
4. He calls himself falsely the Son of God.
5. He calls himself falsely the King of Israel.
6. He entered into the Temple followed by a multitude bearing palm branches in their hands.

Orders the first centurion, Quintus Cornelius, to lead him to the place of execution. Forbids any person whomsoever, either rich or poor, to oppose the death of Jesus Christ.

The witnesses who signed the condemnation of Jesus are:

1. Daniel Robani, a Pharisee
2. Johannes Zorobatel
3. Raphael Robani
4. Capet, a citizen

Jesus shall go out of the city of Jerusalem by the Gate of Struenus [or Struenea].

In the middle of the nineteenth century there was a rumor that the formal death warrant of Jesus had been found in Italy engraved on a copperplate. The text and its story were publicized by an article in the French paper *Le Droit*, probably in the spring of 1839. There was no indication from where it had come but only an affirmation that this must be the most important legal document in

16

229.9
JAM

229
Den

human records. It was soon reprinted in *Gazette de France;* it also received devastating criticism in *Le Moniteur Universel,* for which François Isambert, prominent legal historian, wrote two articles arguing that it was a forgery. It seems that *Le Droit* never cared to answer him.[13]

As often happens in these matters, the criticism was soon forgotten while the story itself survived. In 1849 the article in *Le Droit* was rediscovered in Germany, was translated into German and Swedish, and was spread in a great number of leaflets. The leaflet is, in fact, the usual form of the "death warrant"; the original French text was also circulated in broadsheets and leaflets, and it is probable that it was just such an early print, or a handwritten copy, that came into the hands of the editors of *Le Droit.* There are also early American leaflets, which seem to be based on a French original, perhaps dating earlier than the article in *Le Droit.* One such text was reprinted in William Overton Clough's *Gesta Pilati,* which we shall encounter in a following chapter.

In the various prints the text is always accompanied by the story of its discovery, which goes as follows (with minor variations):

In 1280, some people digging for Roman antiquities in the Italian city of Aquila in the Abruzzi found a copperplate with Hebrew writing. On one side was the death warrant of Jesus; on the other side were the words: "A similar plate is sent to each tribe." This plate was lost but was later rediscovered during the French occupation of Italy (or rather, the Kingdom of Naples) from 1806 to 1815. At that time it was kept in the sacristy of a charterhouse near Naples, where it was enclosed in an ebony box. The discoverer was one of the commissioners of arts who accompanied the French army. Goodspeed doubts that such persons existed, but the story here touches real historic events. During the Napoleonic occupation of Italy, the French took the opportunity to carry away a great number of art treasures for the benefit of the Louvre; the leader of these activities was Dominique Vivant Denon.

According to the story, the French had in mind to seize the copperplate, but the Cartusians managed to prevent it by pointing to the sacrifices that they had made for the French army. From that time the ebony box is said to have been kept in the chapel of Caserta, probably the royal chapel of the Neapolitan kings. Strangely

17

enough, nothing is said about the destiny of the plate, whether it might still be in the box or not. But here comes the important point. A translation of the text of the plate was made, and Denon had a copy made of the plate itself. When his belongings were sold after his death, this copy was bought by a certain Lord Howard for a sum of 2,890 francs. Its further adventures are unknown.

This alleged death warrant and the story about its discovery were never allowed into the scholarly publications of the time, in spite of the great interest in newly found manuscripts such as those of Tischendorf. *The Death Warrant of Jesus* belonged to the more popular literature and has remained so. Today it seems to have been largely forgotten, but it is not impossible that it will be revived again. Such stories have a great ability to survive.

Goodspeed has penetrated into the details of the text, and I see no reason to repeat all his arguments for its lack of authenticity. Let me just make some brief statements: Pilate was never the governor of "lower Galilee," as a Gentile he could not have spoken about Jerusalem as "the holy city," and the dating does not fit either Roman or Jewish calendars. Neither could Pilate have sent copies to the twelve tribes of Israel, for the tribal organization had broken down already in the eighth century B.C. Thus there is no doubt that the text is a forgery.

But when and where and to what purpose was the document produced? Goodspeed thought that it had been forged in the nineteenth century, but this is only partly true. The legend of the find in Aquila has a far longer and more complicated history. It was already known in the sixteenth century, but at that time it was not said to be a copperplate but a parchment scroll. We have, therefore, to take the story from its very beginning.

About the year 1500 among theologians and jurists there arose the favorite topic of who had been guilty of sentencing Jesus to death. Were the Jews responsible for it, as it was often said, or was Pilate the main actor in the drama? The opinions diverged on this point. The New Testament was searched for evidence but with no clear result, for the Gospels never tell us that Pilate had ever pronounced a formal sentence over Jesus. Some hints in this direction were found in the later *Acts of Pilate*. In the debate there sometimes appeared quotations from obscure sources, which we cannot trace any more. Sometimes they may have been free reconstructions, in other cases they may have been taken from some apocryphal writing that is now forgotten.[14]

The debate received new fuel from an alleged discovery, not in Aquila but in Vienne in the south of France, where Pilate is said to have spent the last years of his life. The document, which was printed and quoted in various works, was no real death warrant but rather a kind of confirmation by Pilate that he had sentenced Jesus to death.[15] The document was said to have been found in a box that had been unearthed and to have been written in Latin. The alleged Latin text seems never to have been quoted in the sixteenth century prints, and it is not clear whether it existed at that time. If not the original language would have been French. That it was a forgery was understood already in the middle of the sixteenth century by the learned Bartholomaeus de Salignac.

Several decades later, in 1580, a new version of the death warrant was published. This time it was said to have been found in Aquila in the Abruzzi. The city had not been chosen at random, for in the vicinity was the ancient city of Amiternum, which was regarded as the birthplace of Pilate. Some versions of the find give Amiternum as the source instead of Aquila. The text and its story must have been written just in 1580, when the discovery was said to have been made, for the bishop of the neighboring diocese of Nocera dei Pagani immediately commissioned the jurist Camillo Borello of Naples to investigate the question of its authenticity. In the following year, 1581, he presented a strongly critical statement, in which he declared that the newly found writing was "full of lies." This was certainly correct, for even this time the alleged find was a fraud.

Thanks to Borello's statement, we have access to the original Italian text of the document, which is also confirmed by a few contemporary manuscripts.[16] (There is, of course, no Hebrew original.) The story of the discovery is as follows: the Hebrew document was said to have been found in a ruined wall enclosed in three boxes, one of marble, one of iron, and the outermost of stone. Details of this kind are well known from other similar stories. But it is not clear why this forgery was made. Perhaps it was just another contribution to the debate about the responsibility of Pilate or of the

Jews for the death of Jesus; perhaps somebody wanted to enhance the reputation of Aquila by the find of such a remarkable relic. In the latter case it might be just another parallel to the falsification of more conventional relics.

The text of the death warrant — too lengthy to be reproduced here — has unmistakable similarities to the text of the copperplate. But it is not the same text: the earlier version is far more detailed and has many divergences. It begins with a dating according to no less than eight different chronologies. A great number of reigning princes and officials are enumerated, and not until the second half of the text does the real sentence occur. In its learned verbosity this introduction carries the obvious signs of a Renaissance forgery. Also, the real sentence is more detailed: Pilate determines the text of the board to be fixed on the cross, and the witnesses are no fewer than fifteen persons.

The similarities with the copperplate, however, are also surprisingly numerous. The sentence is dated March 25, Jesus is accused of having entered into the temple amid a palm branch-carrying multitude, the centurion Q[uintus] Cornelius is ordered to take him to the place of execution, Jesus is ordered to be led through a particular gate (here named Zagarola), and everybody is warned against attempting to prevent the execution. Among the witnesses we will recognize Daniel and Joanni; both are *Rabini* (Italian for "rabbis"), later mistaken for a proper name, *Robani*.

There is one point which proves convincingly that the older text was used by the forger of the copperplate. As we have seen, Pilate was described in the latter text as "acting governor of lower Galilee," a province that he had never had any power over (he was governor of Judea and Samaria). In the older text, we find the words "lower Galilee" immediately after Pilate's name, but they are not meant to refer to him but to the next person in the enumeration, Herod Antipas, to whom they are better suited.

Borello's criticism of the older Aquila sentence was not printed until 1588, and at that time the alleged discovery had already been spread far beyond the Italian frontiers. A French translation was published as early as 1581, the year after the alleged discovery.[17] In the same year a German translation was printed, and a Spanish translation caused a sensation in 1583.[18] When the German knight

Melchior Lussy came as a pilgrim to the Holy Land in 1583, he was given something that was said to be the Hebrew text, but the German translation that he carried home had obviously been made from the French. Whatever the learned thought about the document, it had become a public success, which would last for several centuries. This pattern is not entirely unknown in our own time.

We find the Aquila sentence in various forms during the seventeenth and eighteenth centuries, as booklets, as broadsheets or even as an accompanying text for paintings with motifs from the Passion story. But it might be that the enthusiasm for this document petered out by and by. Towards the middle of the nineteenth century it seems to have been forgotten enough to be restored.[19] At this time somebody found it, shortened and rearranged it, and so was able to present it again, this time as the sensational find of a copperplate but still localized to Aquila, the traditional place for the discovery.

But the matter is by no means settled. Here new questions tower aloft, probably without any definite answer. Perhaps the copperplate has never existed but is an invention by the same person who formulated the new text. Or has there been a forged copperplate with the text in question? Or — a third possibility that seems more likely to me — has someone become the owner of a copperplate with Hebrew writing and pretended that it was inscribed with the death warrant of Jesus? To clear up these matters, it would be necessary to carry out extensive research, which would hardly be worthwhile when we know already that this item is nothing but a forgery.

Dominique Vivant Denon was a man strikingly free from scruples, and it is not at all unthinkable that he might have arranged a forgery. But in this case it seems most unlikely. If the story is true so far, Denon only claimed to have received a copy, which he furthermore kept for himself. What interest might he have had for having a forgery made only for his own private use? Imaginable motives are difficult to investigate, as a great deal of Denon's papers are still unpublished, and as there is not yet any comprehensive work on his life and activities.[20]

It is more likely that the fraud is of later date and that Denon's name has only been exploited for the purpose. At the very end of the death warrant there is an oddity that might indicate such an explanation. The last of the witnesses is named Capet, and in the American versions he has the title of "citizen" (in *Le Droit, homme public*). There is a good chance that the original French text may have had *citoyen* here, and that *homme public* is a later accommodation for the French public. For this was no obscure personality. To the French by that time, "the citizen Capet" (French: *Le citoyen Capet*) was extremely well-known but in a totally different context. It was the name that was given to King Louis XVI, when he had been deposed in the French revolution, and it was under this designation that he was sentenced to death. It seems quite absurd that "the citizen Capet" might have been included as a witness under the death warrant of Jesus in a text intended for a French public just a few decades after the revolution.

Here the obscure story of the sale comes into focus, when Lord Howard (whoever he was) is said to have paid a fabulous sum for the alleged copy. The sale of Denon's cabinet took place in 1826, and Isambert was unable to find any reference to the copperplate in the catalogue of the sale. It is therefore possible that the story may refer to some later transaction.

For want of tangible evidence, I allow myself to indulge in lofty speculation. Let us imagine that the whole thing was engineered by a French antiquities dealer who had come into contact with the old death warrant from Aquila! Let us suppose that he is the owner of a copperplate with a Hebrew inscription, and that he would like to sell it. Unfortunately it is not old and verdigrised enough to pass as an original but might be passable as a copy. He then hurries to make a "translation," that is, he takes the sixteenth century text and shortens it so that its length will fit the text of the plate. A suitable story of its discovery is not difficult to concoct for a person who has been dealing with art in Napoleonic France. Then the buyer enters, an English lord with a good fortune, but quite naturally without any knowledge of Hebrew. Here he has the chance of acquiring a unique document, important for entire Christendom, certainly not an original but important anyway! And to be sure, it is the great Denon himself who found it and who had the translation and the copy made. It is also quite possible that the plate, like so many other pieces of art, really belonged to Denon's collection.

So the plate becomes the property of his lordship, and the 2,890 francs move to the dealer's pocket. Indeed, the copperplate with its Hebrew text may still take a place of honor over the mantlepiece in some stately home in Britain.

But what was the role of the citizen Capet in the story? Was it not perhaps just a satanic way of poking fun with the credulous buyer, who may have proved ignorant not only of the Hebrew language but also of French history in a not-too-distant era?

The Protocol of the Sanhedrin is a related document which will only be briefly mentioned in this context, for I do not know how widespread it may have been in English-speaking countries. For three centuries it has enjoyed a great popularity on the European continent, and it is probable that the American reader may have encountered it in one form or another. It is an alleged protocol from the meeting of the Sanhedrin, where the guilt and punishment of Jesus were discussed, and the various councillors expressed their opinions, each in turn.

The twenty statements are all fairly general, and most of the names of the councillors are unknown from the biblical Gospels. Joseph of Arimathea naturally takes the side of Jesus, and the high priest Caiaphas speaks the well-known sentence that it is expedient that one man should die for the people (John 11:50). According to the Gospel these words were uttered at the meeting after the rising of Lazarus, but as we shall see, here they will be connected with the trial of Jesus.

The Protocol of the Sanhedrin belongs to the same literary genre as the older Aquila sentence and originated about the same time, around 1580. It was not mentioned by Borello and may have been produced in Germany. The earliest prints (from 1581) are all of German origin.[21]

The protocol has acquired its great popularity as the standing text for a motif in popular art known as "the sentence of Pilate." Here the two trials of Jesus, before the Sanhedrin and before Pilate, have been compressed into one, so that Caiaphas and Pilate both have their places in the picture. Prints of this kind are known from all parts of the Continent, and some of them must have found their way over the Atlantic Ocean. In the most common version, the

23

councillors are holding large boards with their utterings, rather like the balloons in comic strips.

The Protocol of the Sanhedrin often appears in combination with *The Death Warrant of Jesus,* either in the Vienne version or in the older Aquila version but never with the copperplate version from the nineteenth century. There is no story known about an alleged discovery. In a fairly late print it is stated that the protocol was found in Aquila, but this is certainly a loan from the death warrant.

There are no surprising aspects of the trial of Jesus expressed in this brief text. As the death warrant seems to have been aimed at making Pilate responsible for the sentence, so the protocol may have been aimed at showing how divergent the opinions of the Jews may have been. The idea of letting the councillors speak in turn gives a dramatic effect, and it has been conjectured that the protocol may have had a literary prototype on the stage. A mystery play from Alsfeld in Germany has Pilate surrounded by Jews with various names (but not those used in the protocol), and the text may have originated in a similar context. Throughout its history it has never created any form of sensationalism, but has lived a quiet life as a popular apocryphal writing, in leaflets, broadsheets, and popular art. It also seems unnecessarily severe to give this pious reconstruction the name of forgery. It rather belongs to the genre of popular legends, such as *The Letter of Abgarus.*

5

Leaflets from Heaven

Whosoever worketh on the Sabbath day shall be cursed. I command you to go to church and keep the Lord's Day holy, without any manner of work. You shall not idle or misspend your time in bedecking yourself with superfluities, costly apparel and vain dressing, for I have ordained it a day of rest. I will have that day kept holy, that your sins may be forgiven you.

You shall not break my commandments but observe and keep them, they being written in my own hand and spoken with my own mouth. You shall not only go to church yourself, but also your man servants and your maid servants. Observe my words and learn my commandments. You shall finish your labor every Saturday in the afternoon by six o'clock, at which hour the preparation for the Sabbath begins.

I advise you to fast five days in the year, beginning with Good Friday and continuing the four Fridays following, in remembrance of the five bloody wounds I received for you and all mankind.

You shall diligently and peaceably labor in your respective callings wherein it has pleased God to call you. You shall love one another and cause them that are not baptized to come to church and receive the holy sacraments, baptism, and the Lord's Supper, and to be made members of the church. In so doing I will give you long life and many blessings; your land shall be replenished and bring forth abundance. I will comfort you in the greatest temptations, and surely he that doeth to the contrary shall be cursed. I will also send hardness of heart upon them until I have consumed them, especially upon hardened and impenitent unbelievers.

He that hath given to the poor shall not be unprofited. Remember to keep holy the Sabbath day, for the seventh day have I taken as a resting day to myself.

He that hath a copy of this letter, written in my own hand and spoken with my own mouth, and keepeth it without publishing it to others, shall not prosper, but he that publisheth it to others shall be blessed of me. And if their sins be in number as the stars of the sky, and they truly believe in me, they shall be pardoned. And if they believe not this writing and my commandments, I will send my plagues upon them and consume both you and your children.

Whosoever shall have a copy of this letter and keep it in their house, nothing shall hurt them, and if any woman be in childbirth and put her trust in me, she shall be delivered of her child. You shall hear no more of me but by the Holy Spirit until the Day of Judgment. All goodness and prosperity shall be in the house where a copy of this letter shall be found.

An alleged message from Jesus does not necessarily have to be found in an old manuscript. There are many legends about letters from Jesus that have fallen down from heaven and have been found in the most various places in Europe and Asia. They are usually termed "letters from heaven," and they belong to the most widespread of the apocryphal traditions about Jesus.[22] As Rudolf Stübe has summarized it, they exist in more than twenty European and Oriental languages, they exist in innumerable variants, they extend from India to Iceland and can be traced to Egyptian, Babylonian, and Chinese sources.

I have seen a great number of these variants in German and Scandinavian prints, and in quite a few nineteenth-century Swedish manuscripts. The American prints, which Goodspeed mentions, are hardly accessible in Europe, and the letter quoted above has been taken from Goodspeed's book. In its content, however, it comes very close to the general European type of letter.

As usual, it contains a moralizing hell-fire sermon especially directed to those who profane Sunday; in the American letter quoted, this is called Sabbath, according to Protestant use. The letter thus belongs to the category named "Sunday letters," which is the oldest and most original form. The conclusion of the letter is, as always, filled with promises and threats: the owner of the letter will be protected from various misfortunes, but its despiser will be punished. In this example, fire is not mentioned. Otherwise, one of the reasons for the popularity of the letters was that they were considered to be protection against fire. As late as World War I, heavenly letters were carried by German soldiers as amulets.[23]

With many of the letters there is a story of how the letter was found. It is often said to have been brought to earth by the Archangel Michael; French letters are said to have fallen down on Mont

Saint-Michel, a rocky island near the coast of Brittany. Other letters have fallen down on altars of various churches. The letter quoted is said to have come from Mesopotamia and to have been originally found at the foot of the cross of Jesus. It was hidden under a stone which nobody was able to move, until a child of six or seven years was able to move it without any difficulty. It is a variant of a well-known legend that has been told about King Arthur, which we know from E. T. White's *The Sword in the Stone.* A common version also runs that the letter was hanging in the air and could be copied, but that it withdrew from everyone trying to catch it.

As we have already seen, the letters from heaven have a long history. The first known example appeared in A.D. 584 or 585 on the island of Ibiza among the Balearic Islands.[24] Vincentius, bishop of the island, had come across such a letter; it was said to have fallen on an altar dedicated to St. Peter, but we do not know where. The bishop took the letter seriously and read it publicly in church. Moreover, he sent a copy to Bishop Licinianus of Cartagena in Spain, who was perhaps his superior. Licinianus' reply has been preserved, and here the bishop gives proof of common sense. He deplores that Vincentius had read it to the people, because it was an obvious forgery. We are also given some information about its content, for Licinianus finds its tendency judaizing, and he writes that those who do not go to church on Sunday had better work in their gardens instead of spending the day dancing. The last sentence seems to be related to the general polemic against Jewish customs; the Jews were often accused by the Christians of having too much fun on the Sabbath day.

The keeping of Sunday as a day of rest is no early Christian rule. In its rigorous form it seems to have been preached for the first time in southern France, perhaps under the impact of the many Jews who lived there in harmony with the Christian population. The provincial council of Mâcon in 585 (in the same year that the letter appeared in Ibiza) rejected all unnecessary work on Sunday and proclaimed the Jewish Sabbath as an Old Testament prototype for Christian Sunday-keeping.[25]

There is a common exhortation in the heavenly letters, as in the letter quoted, that Sunday has to be celebrated from Saturday evening, just as the Jewish Sabbath begins on Friday evening at sunset. Several councils in the seventh and eighth centuries decided that Sunday had to be celebrated in this way. The heavenly letters thus agree with the new ideals for Sunday-keeping that were spread from France to the Continent in general during the Dark Ages. It is therefore probable that the letters were intended for propagating these customs in the Church.

Soon enough, however, the letters lost their original aim. Probably it was not their content that made them popular, but the fascinating thought that they had "fallen down" from heaven and were written by Jesus with his own hand. The letters from heaven, which soon took on the most various shapes, became a popular literature, generally rejected by the church and by the worldly powers. The Lateran Council of 745 condemned the letters as heretical; Charlemagne and his son Louis the Pious also condemned them, but they nevertheless spread all over the Continent and further to Britain, to Ireland, and to Iceland. German letters are known from the 1260s; in Scandinavia they do not appear until after the Reformation. In the Orient the letters also achieved great popularity. There are versions in Greek, Armenian, Syriac, and Karshuni (Arabic written with Syriac characters), and it is possible that all are imitations of the French and Spanish letters.[26]

As the official Church repudiated the letters, they became a mighty factor in the many popular movements of the Middle Ages. When Pope Urban II summoned Christendom to the First Crusade in 1096, there appeared a prophet named Peter the Hermit who preached this duty to the masses in France. He pretended to have been to the Church of the Holy Sepulchre in Jerusalem, and there to have received a letter from Christ himself, commissioning him to his task. When the unofficial Crusade of the Shepherds was preached in 1251, one of the leaders was a renegade monk known as "The Master of Hungary." He had received a letter from the Virgin Mary, who had appeared to him in a host of angels, and he always carried this letter with him. Still more important was perhaps another heavenly letter, spread by the flagellant movement in Germany from about 1261. A shining marble tablet had descended over the Holy Sepulchre in Jerusalem, and an angel had read the message written by God's own hand. This letter, in which the profanation of Sunday was properly condemned, became a constant source of inspiration as the flagellant processions moved about Germany throughout the thirteenth and fourteenth centuries. When the Reformation began, other similar letters were produced, denouncing the pope and propagating the new religious ideas. In the Protestant countries during the following centuries, the letters became more popular than ever, as they spread apocalyptic ideas, especially in times of war and misfortune.

The letters from heaven differ from most of the apocrypha we discuss by their total lack of pseudoscientific pretensions. They are related instead to the religious concept common in all the ancient cultures with written documents, that a message can be given to humanity by a book or a letter descending from heaven.

We know a number of such heavenly books believed to have communicated revelations to man. In early Christian times, the Judeo-Christian sect known as the Elchesaites possessed such a book, which had been given to them by an angel from heaven. A far more important example is certainly the Koran, which Mohammed received from the hand of the Archangel Gabriel. According to Islamic faith, the original of the Koran is in heaven, and the writing communicated by Mohammed is only a copy, read from the original by the prophet. The same motif is to be found in the *Gospel of Barnabas,* with its evident Islamic tendency; here Gabriel carries the heavenly Gospel down to Jesus. A more modern analogy is the *Book of Mormon;* it was written on golden plates and brought to Joseph Smith by the angel Moroni, who called for the plates when the translation had been finished. In this case the original is also inaccessible. The revelations of *The Gospel of the Holy Twelve* and of *The Aquarian Gospel* belong to the same tradition, even if they are lacking some of the well-known mythological features.[27]

This is no place for a broad reflection about the phenomenon of the heavenly book or the heavenly letter. Generally, it may be seen as just one type of legend about the marvelous book discovery found in so many modern apocrypha. The psychological background of all these book stories is evidently quite similar. Is it not simply the expectation of finding a new revelation, more definitive and more correct than that of the New Testament? The revelation may not be handed down from heaven, but there is the hope that it might be hidden here on earth in a manuscript, hitherto unknown.

6

The Angel with the Golden Plates

None of the books presented here have been as much discussed as *The Book of Mormon.* I will, therefore, restrict myself to summarizing the results of other writers and evaluating their arguments to the best of my ability. This is a delicate matter, for *The Book of Mormon,* as well as the other writings of Joseph Smith, are believed to be divine revelation within the community named The Church of Jesus Christ of Latter-day Saints, and known in common speech as the Mormon Church. To criticize a holy book is to attack the faith of others, and I know that some things that I write here may be taken in that way. I have no aversion towards the Mormon Church, and the Mormons I have encountered have been strikingly open and sympathetic people. But truth is dearer to me, as said Aristotle about his friendship with Plato, and I am convinced that *The Book of Mormon* has elements connecting it with the history of Bible forgery.[28]

Many have had some contact with this book, which is spread by the polite and neat young men who are the missionaries of the Mormon Church. Not as many have read through this heavy book — its size is about a third of the Bible — but many may have observed that its layout and typography are similar to those of our Bibles. It is printed in double columns and divided into books, chapters, and verses in the established way. The names of the books, however, are different from those of the Bible: First and Second Book of Nephi, Book of Jacob, Book of Enos, Book of Jarom, Book of Omni, The Words of Mormon, Book of Mosiah, Book of Alma, Book of Helaman, Third and Fourth Nephi, Book of Mormon, Book of Ether, and Book of Moroni.

The origin of *The Book of Mormon* is a remarkable and often told story, which I will only summarize briefly. Joseph Smith

31

(1805–1844) belonged to a poor family with little education; at the beginning of the story, the family had settled in Palmyra, New York. At the age of fourteen, Joseph was said to have already had his first revelation. It was not until three years later, in 1823, that he heard about *The Book of Mormon* for the first time.[29] An angel came into his bedroom and announced that his name was Moroni. He said that there was a hidden book written on golden plates, which held the history of the earlier inhabitants of the American continent. In this book it was also told that Jesus had visited America after his resurrection, and that he had also founded his Church here. The plates were written in "reformed Egyptian," but with them there was a breastplate with the "Urim and Thummim," the sacred stones of the Israelite high priest, and with their help Joseph would be able to perform the translation.

Directed by the angel, Joseph went to a hill, named Cumorah, near Manchester, New York; there he found the golden plates enclosed in a stone box. Before he was allowed to take care of them, he had to go through a probationary period. Not until September 22, 1827, did the angel hand over the plates to him along with the commandment to keep them well and to translate them. When the translation had been made, the angel came back and called for the plates. From that day no one has seen them, but it is the belief of the Mormons that they are buried somewhere in Cumorah. It was only two thirds of the plates that Smith was allowed to translate; the remaining third has not yet been revealed.

The first edition of *The Book of Mormon* was printed in 1830; it has since been published in innumerable editions in many languages. The book is in the form of a chronicle extending from the building of the Tower of Babel until the beginning of the fifth century A.D. The earliest history of how Jared and his family sailed in eight ships over the ocean after the confusion of tongues in Babel is told only in the Book of Ether towards the end of the collection. Otherwise, the main story runs chronologically through *The Book of Mormon*. This main history is introduced by the story of how Lehi and his family left Jerusalem about 600 B.C. and sailed to America. His three sons, Nephi, Laman, and Lemuel, later became the ancestors of the two peoples that the book describes, the good and law-abiding Nephites and the wicked Lamanites, to whom the descendants of Lemuel also belong.

This chronicle mostly reminds us of the historical books of the Old Testament, but later on in the collection, in Third and Fourth Nephi, a "New Testament" part describes the arrival of Christ in the New World. After his resurrection he is said to have visited the people of the Nephites and to have founded his Church among them. This church existed for a few hundred years, until the Lamanites managed to destroy the Nephites forever. The traditions were saved by the prophet Mormon, who wrote them down on golden plates from earlier records. His son, Moroni, buried them in the soil of Cumorah in A.D. 421. Transformed into an angel, he was later able to show Joseph Smith the way to the site and later to deliver the plates to him.

The general opinion among non-Mormons is that *The Book of Mormon* is a creation of Joseph Smith himself, a position which is also my own. The supernatural circumstances of the discovery arouse the skepticism of the outsider, but also the style and content of the book prove that it is not an ancient file of documents but a work from Smith's own time.

Many statements in *The Book of Mormon* are quite contrary to our knowledge of the early conditions of America. Despite Thor Heyerdahl's adventurous voyages at sea, it seems quite certain that the first inhabitants of the continent came by land over the Bering Strait. The zoological statements in *The Book of Mormon* are often quite impossible. For instance, it is said that the Jaredites met "sheep and swine and elephants and cureloms and cumoms". (The presence of the last two species cannot be denied, of course, as nobody seems to know to what the words might refer). Likewise, Nephi, at his landing, found the forests filled with "cows, oxen, asses, and horses." Weapons of steel are mentioned; yet iron was unknown in America before the arrival of Columbus.[30]

The Book of Mormon also contains unmistakable allusions to American society in the nineteenth century. There are harsh attacks on the Catholic Church, which was often described as the "Babylonic whore." Anti-Catholic sentiment in America would reach its height about ten years after the book was printed, but the church was already a growing force then, represented by Irish immigrants. Freemasons are also attacked in *The Book of Mormon,* slightly disguised as "Gadianton's robbers." At a later stage in his life, Smith would take a more friendly attitude towards them.[31]

There is little autobiographical matter in the *Book of Mormon,* for Smith seems to have restrained his own personality in a conscious way. But there is a Smith family story in Lehi's long dream, told in First Nephi 8.[32] According to Joseph's mother, this dream was one that her husband had dreamt in 1811. Only that chapter has a bit of the visionary power otherwise missing in *The Book of Mormon.*

The Book of Mormon is not pleasurable reading—"chloroform in print" is Mark Twain's familiar verdict. The wording is stereotyped, the events monotonous. The course of events as such could be the stuff of a magnificent epic, had it come into the hands of the right author. But Joseph Smith was no Tolkien; there is no epic breadth here, no exciting characters, no moving events or fanciful scenes. The whole thing jogs along at the same pace as in the driest possible style of the Old Testament chronicles. The language is heavy footed with the King James Version as its pattern; long passages are taken directly from this translation. But *The Book of Mormon* is a poor imitation with its stereotyped language. It has been estimated that the words "and it came to pass" are found in it about 2,000 times.

The Book of Mormon pretends to be a translation, but it has been done in a supernatural way. Almost nothing exists of the alleged original in "reformed Egyptian." According to Smith, the name *Mormon* comes from Egyptian, from *more mon,* or "more good." But *more* seems rather to be English, and no Egyptian word *mon* with the meaning of "good" is known. Smith wrote down proofs of the characters, but they bear no similarity to Egyptian hieroglyphics.[33]

Much labor has been undertaken in order to find literary prototypes of *The Book of Mormon.* There is no reason to discuss the widespread Spaulding-Rigdon theory any more. According to this, Smith had taken his story from an unpublished novel by a certain Solomon Spaulding, and Smith's later fellow-worker Sidney Rigdon was the intermediary link. Nobody has ever been able to produce the alleged novel manuscript, and the historic course of events makes it impossible that Rigdon could have played any role when *The Book of Mormon* was first written.[34]

There was much other literature, however, from which Smith might have gotten his inspiration. The origin of American Indians was a favorite topic of speculation; many liked to think that they might be the descendants of the ten lost tribes of Israel. Smith may have gotten his idea from a book on this theme, written by a Rev. Ethan Smith in Vermont and published in 1823.[35] But if that is so, he cannot be accused of plagiarism. The idea of transplanting the history of the Old Testament to America seems to be entirely Smith's own.

There is an interesting possibility, which has been pointed out by the Swedish scholar Åke V. Ström, that Smith might have adopted elements of the religious traditions of the Delawares, which have some remarkable parallels to *The Book of Mormon*.[36] Especially striking is the comparison with the yearly chronicle of the Lenni Lennapi Indians, which was carved into wooden tables and painted with red. The chronicle, which was written with a kind of pictograms, began at the sea on the West Coast and related the Indians' journey eastwards. It is a strange feature of *The Book of Mormon* that both Jared and Lehi are said to have sailed over the Pacific, not over the Atlantic Ocean; the latter alternative would seem to have been more natural to Smith, who lived relatively close to the East Coast. The idea of Jesus' appearance in America may also have been inspired by Indian myths about their cultural heroes, who sometimes remind one of Jesus, and whose myths may in turn have been colored by Christian influence. There is no evidence, however, pointing to a direct contact between Smith and the Indians of his region.

The Book of Mormon is no ordinary literary forgery, but occupies a peculiar place between revelation and alleged book discovery. This dual character is present even in Smith's own personality and in his wish to be prophet and finder at the same time. He found his golden plates in a box buried in Cumorah, but when he finally got them into his hands, then it was the angel who delivered them. He performed his translation not in the usual way but by looking into transparent stones just as a fortune-teller uses a crystal ball.

While doing the translation, he received other revelations directly from God, and these continued throughout his lifetime. The most important of these were gathered into a book named *Doctrine and Covenants*, which is one of the most important documents of the Mormon Church. Leaders of the church after Smith have also received similar revelations.

At the same time as Joseph Smith was translating *The Book of Mormon*, he also received the revelation of a New Testament fragment, which he communicated to his secretary, Oliver Cowdery. It was said to be a manuscript on parchment, which had been written by the apostle John and hidden by him; it was now revealed directly to Smith, who had no need of the manuscript itself.[37] The brief text, part of the last chapter of the Fourth Gospel, has been included in *Doctrine and Covenants* as chapter 7. Like *The Book of Mormon* the "fragment" has a dual provenance: it is a manuscript hidden here on earth and inaccessible to us, and it has also been communicated to the "editor" in a supernatural way. We will find the same duality in *The Gospel of the Holy Twelve,* an alleged Tibetan document, which is said to have been communicated to the editor G. J. R. Ouseley in visions and with the assistance of spirits.

The story of the preservation of the plates and the way the translation was made shows us clearly how Smith took the double role of editor and revealer. His first secretary was his wife, Emma, who has herself described the proceedings.[38] She was totally forbidden to see the plates, but they often rested on the table wrapped in a piece of cloth, and it happened that she touched them while she was dusting; on these occasions they felt pliable like thick paper and would rustle with a metallic sound. Joseph had no immediate need of the plates for his translation but had only to look into his stones; it is said that he used the Urim and Thummim for the first 116 pages (they were later lost); for the rest he used a little black stone.

Emma Smith was soon replaced as secretary by Martin Harris, an enthusiastic follower of Smith who was later to finance the publication of *The Book of Mormon*. The room was now divided with a blanket. On one side Joseph Smith was translating by looking into his stones; on the other side sat Harris, transcribing Smith's dictation at a table. It was strictly forbidden for Harris to

try to see the plates or Joseph during his work. The next secretary
was Oliver Cowdery, who worked under the same conditions.
David Whitmer, who visited them during their work, tells us that
Smith had the stone in his hat, which he held tightly to his face
in order to keep out all light. In the darkness the writing then
became visible as if on a piece of parchment.[39]

It may seem as if the plates were quite unnecessary, since Smith
would receive the revelation anyway in a direct way. But to Smith
himself the plates were of great importance. They were the foundation for his claims to having rediscovered those ancient traditions
which the children of Israel had left behind in the New World. Also,
for later generations of Mormons the existence of the plates is a cor-
nerstone of their doctrine. The editions of *The Book of Mormon*
always contain two testimonies from those who claim to have seen
the plates: one by the three assistants Cowdery, Whitmer, and
Harris; the other one by eight members of the families of Whitmer
and Smith.[40]

It was not during the course of their work, however, that the
two secretaries and Whitmer were allowed to see the plates. For
in their testimony it is said that "an angel of God came down from
heaven, and he brought and laid before our eyes, that we beheld
and saw the plates, and the engravings thereon." According to common sense, it was thus in a vision and not with their corporeal eyes
that they saw the golden plates. Their statement is also confirmed
by Joseph Smith's own account of the event. The vision is said to
have taken place in a wood where he and the three witnesses had
withdrawn in order to pray and to have the promise fulfilled that
they would bear the testimonies about the plates. Why they should
set out for the wood at the same time as the plates were in Smith's
home is one of the many obscurities that call for explanation.[41]

The second testimony is still more concretely expressed. It says
"that Joseph Smith, Jun., the translator of this work, has shown
us the plates of which hath been spoken, which have the appearance
of ancient work, and of curious workmanship. And this we bear
record with words of soberness, that the said Smith has shown unto
us, for we have seen and hefted, and know of surety that the said
Smith has got the plates of which he have spoken."

Testimony in such serious terms and with such concrete wording seems to have a great weight. But in face of this testimony the questions accumulate. When did the witnesses see the plates? Was it at the same time or on different occasions? Joseph Smith, who has so much to say about the first three witnesses and their vision of the plates, even stating that the three were elected by God to see them, has nothing to say about the other eight witnesses. If so many were allowed to see and touch the plates, why then should it be forbidden for Emma Smith, and why was there need of an angel from heaven to enable the three to see them? There has never been a satisfying answer to these questions, but it has often been guessed that Joseph Smith manipulated those around him in one way or another. It is certain, however, that the eight were firmly convinced about the existence of the plates; it is not impossible to conclude that the enthusiastic convictions of the group made the members ready to sign the testimony, even if they were conscious of the fact that they had never actually seen the plates.

The discovery of the golden plates was the all-pervading event in the circle around Joseph Smith, and it gave meaning to the life of all. Even when the circle was disrupted by internal strife, the unreserved faith in the plates remained. All of the first three witnesses subsequently left Smith's community, even though Cowdery and Harris finally returned. There were many who tried to make them confess that it had all been an invention by Smith. But all such attempts failed; the three remained certain of the existence of the plates, however much they became disappointed in Smith. On his deathbed Martin Harris is said to have exclaimed, "Book, book, book!" The fascination of the marvelous book could not be dispelled by any means.[42]

In spite of the plates, *The Book of Mormon* is above all a revelation with Joseph Smith as the personal receiver. Some of the stranger details can be explained by Smith's earlier history, which is not so willingly told by the Mormons. In the environment in which Joseph grew up, there was a great interest in stories about hidden treasures, and there was a general belief that they could be detected by crystal-gazing. Joseph spent some time with such activities, obviously with a certain success, even if he later said that he had received "only fourteen dollars a month for it."[43]

Many stories told about young Joseph Smith may be dismissed

as malevolent slander. But not all of them can be discounted, for we get a clear picture of Smith's early activities in a court record that has survived. On March 20, 1826, he was taken before the justice of the peace in Bainbridge, Chenango County, New York, and accused as "a disorderly person and an impostor." Smith declared before the court that he had been looking for gold deposits underground, and that he used a special stone in his search. He also used the stone for finding buried treasure and lost items, and several witnesses confirmed this. One witness, Horace Stowel, said that he had seen Smith look through a stone into his hat in order to find out where a chest of dollars had been buried. Another witness, Arad Stowel, said that Smith had demonstrated his ability for him: Smith had laid a book upon a white cloth and had placed himself with his back towards the book; then he had read from the book by holding a white, translucent stone towards a burning candle. These practices are strikingly similar to those employed in the translation of *The Book of Mormon.*

Immediately after *The Book of Mormon* had been finished, Smith set about working on his next great task, revising the Bible according to his revelations. This time there was no need of an alleged document, since all flowed from his inspiration. This work was never finished; after Smith's death in 1844 the unfinished manuscript became the property of Emma Smith. It finally came into the possession of the branch of Mormonism called The Reorganized Church, which still owns some of the most important documents of the movement. The revised Bible was not published until 1867, and has never been fully accepted by the great Mormon Church in Utah.[44] The "revision" mainly consists of interpolations of verses, such as this prophecy about Joseph Smith himself inserted into Genesis 50:

> Thus saith the Lord God of my fathers unto me, A choice seer will I raise up out of the fruit of thy loins, . . . and his name shall be called Joseph, and it shall be after the name of his father. [Smith's father was also named Joseph.]

In Isaiah 29 we find an inserted prophecy about *The Book of Mormon,* too lengthy to be reproduced here in full. I here only quote a few sentences:

> And it shall come to pass, that the Lord God shall bring forth
> unto you the words of a book; and they shall be the words of them
> which have slumbered . . . But the book shall be delivered unto a
> man, and he shall deliver the words of the book . . . And there is
> none other which shall view it, save it be a few according to the
> will of God, to bear testimony of his word unto the children of men.

Later Joseph Smith gradually changed his role of discoverer to
that of prophet. He returned to the discoverer's role once more,
however, under new conditions. In the summer of 1835, when
Smith and his faithful had founded a new center in Kirtland, Ohio,
the town was visited by an itinerant exhibitor of curiosities. He had
with him four Egyptian mummies and two papyri; he wanted
Smith to help him with the translation of the papyri, for Smith had
already made himself known as the translator of *The Book of Mormon* from "reformed Egyptian." One should keep in mind that there
was no one in America at the time who had learned to decipher
Egyptian hieroglyphics. Champollion had already published his
famous interpretation of the Rosetta stone and of other Egyptian
inscriptions, but it would take several decades more before the
art of reading ancient Egyptian had penetrated into the learned
world. Anyway, the papyri soon became the property of Smith,
and after some study he declared that one of them was written by
Abraham, and that the other was about Joseph in Egypt. The Joseph
papyrus was never heard of again, but *The Book of Abraham* was
translated by Smith and is now part of *The Pearl of Great Price*,
which is considered one of the normative documents of the Mormons, together with *The Book of Mormon* and *Doctrine and
Covenants.*[45]

Interested Egyptologists could soon demonstrate that Smith's interpretation of the papyri was pure fantasy. Doubts were also expressed about the authenticity of the papyri themselves. In 1966,
however, the papyri were rediscovered by Professor Aziz S. Atiya
in the Metropolitan Museum in New York. They were later
delivered to N. Eldon Tanner, one of the highest leaders of the Mormon Church. The rediscovery has been followed by a lively discussion within the Mormon Church on how Smith's interpretations
may be reconciled with those of Egyptologists. I have somewhere
seen the explanation that *The Book of Abraham* was communicated

by direct inspiration, like so many of Smith's revelations, but that the papyrus had served as a kind of catalyst, a means of releasing the revelation. In that case, similar questions may be raised about *The Book of Mormon,* for cannot the alleged plates be considered as analogous objects, the outward manifestation of a reality that was in fact of a mental nature?

Wolfgang Speyer called *The Book of Mormon* a specimen of "genuine religious pseudepigraphy." Krister Stendahl takes a similar approach in calling it a counterpart of the Jewish Targum, an adaption of biblical matter for a certain historic situation.[46] In this way it is possible to give *The Book of Mormon* a kind of legitimacy as a late Christian apocryphon. Whatever may be said about the literary value of the book, it would certainly be unjust to deny its religious impact. It has inspired generations of faithful to a forceful religious activity, and it has given them a conviction that many other Christians might envy.

A great deal of this impact may be derived from that of Joseph Smith himself. He had a prophetic quality, which was perhaps the most important constituent of his complicated personality. His appearance as a prophet of God has the mark of religious conviction. Also, there is nothing reprehensible in the fact that his revelations often crossed the border between inspiration and conscious reflection; the same may be said about a great number of religious visionaries and prophets through the ages. It is an unanswered question whether his dictation of *The Book of Mormon* took place in some state of trance, and had the character of an automatic message.[47]

Had Joseph Smith been satisfied with his role of prophet, he would have made it easier for posterity to accept him as a somewhat odd but respectable preacher. The dubious element in his makeup is seen in his dual role of revealer and discoverer. From his youth he cherished dreams of finding hidden treasures by supernatural means, and the dream of making the marvelous book discovery prevailed to such an extent that he became overly entangled in obscure translations of the more or less real books he claimed to have found. It is this side of his activity that puts him among those who have presented alleged documents without sufficient evidence for their high pretensions.

41

7

Those Versatile Essenes

I have informed you of all these things, my Brethren, that you shall indeed know that Jesus was our Brother, and belonged to our Holy Order.

Thus all doubts and uncertainties on this matter must be ended. Jesus, our Brother, willingly suffered death that he might thereby glorify the doctrines of our Order; and the greatest reward of our virtue is that we may, in like manner, be allowed to sacrifice ourselves for it.

You have heard the accounts which the Jews and his disciples have given concerning him; that they have seen him in the mountains and on the road after they believed him to be dead.

The divine providence has given us a minute knowledge of these events that is hidden from the people, and it is our duty to inform you of the facts in reply to your questions relative hereto.

Even as I write this, my eyes overflow with tears, and I seem to see our Brother in the midst of his torture and in the anguish of death; and my afflicted mind is anew wounded by the recollection of his majestic courage and self-sacrifice.

He was sent of God, chosen by the Almighty, beloved of us all, and inspired both in teaching and in the knowledge of nature and its elements.

Hear then, my Brethren, what occured in Jerusalem seven passovers ago. I have seen it all with my own eyes, and with my lips I have kept it a secret, that the world should not know it; for the Jews and the heathen believe only in the things they have seen with their eyes. And so they have no faith in God beyond that which they can conceive with their senses.

> *The Essene Letter*
> (*The Crucifixion by an Eye-Witness*,
> pp. 54–55)

The alleged document quoted here has been published in English under various titles such as *The Crucifixion by an Eye-Witness* (1907), *The Crucifixion and the Resurrection of Jesus, by an Eye-Witness* (1919), and *An Eye-Witness Account* (1975). I prefer to

give it the more handy title *The Essene Letter,* which covers the
pretentions of the writing fairly well. The quotation is taken from
the 1907 edition, which is most unsatisfying but the only one I could
obtain in English translation.[48]

Many have believed that this letter is an authentic account of
the crucifixion of Jesus. It has often been used as a basis for
hypotheses that Jesus never died on the cross but was rescued in
secret. As we can see from the quotation, the letter pretends to have
been written by a member of the order of the Essenes; from the
context it is also clear that it is meant to be a report from the Essenes
in Jerusalem to their brothers in Alexandria. The letter is said to
have been written seven years after the crucifixion of Jesus. It tells
us that Jesus was a member of the Essene order and that he knew
its secrets, which mainly consisted of various remedies for illness.

The main point of the story concerns the crucifixion of Jesus and
the following events. Jesus, says the letter, only apparently died
on the cross and was taken down in a most exhausted condition.
He was revived by Joseph of Arimathea and Nicodemus, who had
access to the secret art of healing practiced by the Essenes. Thus
Jesus was able to appear to his disciples, who were excluded from
the secrets of the order, and who believed that he had risen from
the dead. The angel at the tomb of Jesus and the two angels at the
Ascension were merely Essene brothers dressed in white. A run-
ning theme in the story is that the brothers were the really
knowledgeable ones and the leaders of the course of events, while
the disciples were uniformed and credulous, seeing wonders in
events that the initiated knew to have natural causes. According
to the story, Jesus did not survive for a long time, but died after
six months from the effects of his torture.

The Essene Letter has a German origin, and it was first published in Leipzig in 1849. It was accompanied by another writing,
published in the same year, which told about the childhood and
youth of Christ.[49] This second book, which never became as popular
as the letter, does not seem to have ever been translated into English.
We will return later to the original history of these two books, and
begin by looking into the contents of the letter.

When *The Essene Letter* first appeared, very little was known
about the Essenes. The only existent information consisted of scat-

tered evidence in the writings of the Jewish authors Philo and Josephus, and of the Roman author Pliny the Elder. It was only about a century after publication of the letter, that our knowledge of the Essenes was dramatically increased by the discovery of the Dead Sea Scrolls.[50] Scholars soon realized that the ancient owners of the scrolls — generally called the Qumran sect — were actually the Essenes or were at least closely related to them. There is good reason to believe that some of the Qumran documents have an Essene origin, and there is thus an abundance of comparison material for the letter.

A comparison with the Dead Sea Scrolls immediately discloses that *The Essene Letter* is no genuine writing from the order of the Essenes. First of all, it is said to have been written in Latin, but the real Essenes wrote in Hebrew and in Aramaic; not a single Latin fragment has been found among the Dead Sea documents. Although the alleged addressees, the brethren in Alexandria, would probably have spoken Greek, Latin was never used at that time among Jews in the eastern part of the Roman Empire.

It is content and style, however, that firmly unmask the author as a nineteenth-century rationalist with romantic inclinations. It is perfectly clear that his sporadic knowledge of the Essenes all comes from the literature accessible in the nineteenth century. As far as I can see, all his information could have been derived from Josephus. The white robes often mentioned in the letter are also mentioned by Josephus.[51] The interest in "the secrets of nature, and the influence of herbs and stones on the human body" also comes from Josephus, who does not, however, make it into such a main point. In *The Essene Letter* the members of the order are described as representatives of the Enlightenment from about 1800, benevolent and rationalist nature-healers. Not only are miracles and angels dismissed as popular superstition: God, the Mosaic Law, the prophets and the people of Israel have all been pushed into the background. These matters, however, were essential to the real Essenes, as far as we may judge from the Qumran texts. In Qumran, the study of Old Testament writings was a dominant part of life, and there was a great interest in the fulfilment of the prophecies in the expected eschatological events. About these matters *The Essene Letter* has nothing to tell us.

The real Essenes were Jews. They would never have considered speaking about "the Jews" as a foreign people. But this is exactly what the letter does in the quoted passage, speaking about "the Jews and the heathen." This expression (where "Gentiles" would certainly be a better translation than "heathen") arose at the time when the Christian Church began to think of itself as "a third people" beside the Jews and the Gentiles.

The whole letter has a romantic tone, in no respect resembling the style of Jewish writings from the beginning of our era. It appears that the author was fond of natural scenery. Here is an example:

> And Jesus led them to the place most dear to him, near the summit of Mount Olivet, where can be seen almost the whole of the land of Palestine; for Jesus longed once more to look upon the country where he had lived and worked.
>
> To the east was seen Jordan, the Dead Sea and the Arabian Mountains; and to the west shone the fires from the Temple Rock; but on the other side of the mountain was Bethania. . . .
>
> And he exhorted his disciples to be of good cheer, and firm in their faith. As he spoke his voice grew more and more melancholy, and his mind was absorbed in solemn transport.
>
> He prayed for the friends he was about to leave, and lifting his arms he blessed them. And the mist rose around the mountain, tinted by the descending sun [p. 123f.].

The author reveals his falseness further, however, when he forgets that he should live in the 30s A.D. and begins to speak about the situation as if it were the past:

> Inasmuch as the Pharisees held rigidly to the traditions and details of the law of Moses, they were deeply aggrieved against every one who did not keep in outward form to the ceremonials of their temple service [page 44].

This is meant to have been written in Jerusalem seven years after the crucifixion of Jesus, at a time when there were still as many Pharisees in the city as before!

The new Christian community is also described in the same absurd past tense: "Therefore faithfully they kept together and daily went to the temple and to the places where he had taught them" (page 125). It is obvious that the author was influenced here by

Acts 2:46. In the original German text, even the Essenes are spoken of in the same past tense and in the third person, even though they were the senders as well as the addressees of the letter.

Apart from certain main interests of the author (the Essene order and its nature remedies, the white robes, the initiation ceremonies, and especially the rescuing of Jesus), there is hardly anything here that has not been taken from the four canonical Gospels. It is striking that no personal names appear except those known from the Gospels. Because the Essene author is anonymous, this lack of names contributes to the poor impression. The natural scenery excepted, there is not a hint of local color. The corresponding book about the birth and childhood of Jesus, however, introduces a new personality, the Essene Euphanias, who becomes the real father of Jesus, and who has been committed to this task by the Essenes. Here, as always in these two books, the main idea is that all the miracles of the Bible must be attributed to natural causes, and that the secret Essene brotherhood has to be represented as the real agent behind the seemingly miraculous course of events.

One point that clearly exposes the author is his knowledge of the four canonical Gospels, which were not written down until the second half of the first century, and were never combined into a group of four until the second half of the second century. In the letter, the evangelists are named John, Matthew, Mark, and Luke in the traditional way, just as if they had been the accepted authors of the Gospels in the 30s, when none of the Gospels had yet been written! When he mentions Mark, moreover, the author also mentions the unauthentic close of the Gospel, which is dated to the second century. This clearly proves that *The Essene Letter* is a forgery.

The story about the discovery of the letter is certainly as much a concoction as the letter itself. According to "the German translator," the Latin parchment scroll with the letter was found in a forgotten monastery library in Alexandria. Orthodox fanatics and intriguing Jesuits had managed to prevent the French academy from becoming the owners of the scroll, which was even in danger of being destroyed. A copy, however, was rescued from "Orthodox fools" by "Pythagorean Societies." By chance, it became the property of a German brotherhood which was the last remnant of the old Essene wisdom. The letter had thus, after two thousand years, come home to its own people who had then made the translation. It goes without saying that this romantic tale does not deserve any credence.

In 1849 when the letter was first published, an alert theologian, Johann Nepomuk Truelle, had found out how *The Essene Letter* had come into existence.[52] He could prove convincingly that the "letter" was a plagiarism of a well-known Jesus novel from 1800. In detail after detail the action conforms to that of the novel. The novel by Karl Heinrich Venturini was not without precedent either. Behind it lay an entire literature from the Era of Enlightenment, which attempted to make Jesus an Essene and a nature-healer in the spirit of rationalism.

If we want to trace the history of *The Essene Letter* from the very beginning, we must go back to the first decades of the eighteenth century, and the beginning of rationalist enlightenment theology. After the fall of the Stuarts in England in 1689, rationalism quickly became a topic of general debate, and neither the New Testament nor the personality of Jesus was excepted from criticism based on the primacy of reason. The leading principle was that Christianity could not contain anything contrary to reason. Many theologians, therefore, wanted to discount the miracles of Jesus and the accounts of the resurrection. They showed great inventiveness in searching for "natural causes."

The eighteenth century, however, was not only an era of skepticism. The romanticism of secret societies flourished, and Freemasons, Rosicrucians, and Illuminates found sympathy with the higher levels of society as never before or later. Perhaps the natural secret of Jesus was that he had been initiated as the brother of a secret society: this was an attractive thought for many, satisfying reason as well as romantic sentiment. The most likely society was the Essene order, known from antiquity, and so the idea of Jesus the Essene was born.[53] As early as 1717, the English dean Humphrey Prideaux reported that the deists had observed the similarity between the New Testament and the Essene doctrines, and that they drew the conclusion that Christianity was a branch of the Essene community.

Such ideas were spread all over the European continent from England. In Germany, radical criticism of the established concept

47

of Jesus came from Hermann Samuel Reimarus, who depicted Jesus as a political revolutionary, and who said that the disciples had stolen his body.[54] There began heated debate at the German universities; here also, the idea took form that Jesus had perhaps been an Essene.

The first author known to have written seriously about this assumption was an adventurous Prussian theologian named Karl Friedrich Bahrdt (1741–1792), who was for a short time a highly popular lecturer at the University of Halle. Like so many others, he found the biblical account of Jesus irreconcilable with reason and, therefore, rewrote the history of Jesus in a way quite similar to *The Essene Letter*.[55] He described Nicodemus and Joseph of Arimathea as Essenes, and said that the aim of their order was to raise the people from the simple Messianic faith to a higher level of knowledge. Supposedly Jesus and his disciples were also initiated into the order, but because the disciples were never initiated into the highest degree, they were unable to comprehend the teachings of Jesus. Neither did they understand that the miracles of Jesus had been engineered by the Essene brethren. According to Bahrdt, Jesus was only apparently dead on the cross, and Joseph of Arimathea managed to restore him to life through the art of healing. The angel at the tomb was supposedly an Essene brother dressed in white. Towards the end of Bahrdt's novel, Jesus withdrew into solitude but encountered Paul on the road to Damascus.

The work of Karl Heinrich Venturini (1768–1849) followed that of Bahrdt.[56] Like Bahrdt, Venturini was a minister and a disciple of the Enlightenment, and he took it upon himself to improve Bahrdt's story. His novel was published in four volumes and became the prototype for several later Jesus novels. The author of *The Essene Letter* condensed the contents of Venturini's novel into the size of a booklet and gave it the form of a letter. In this manner, the story of Jesus the Essene could be legitimated as a real discovery.

It is no accident that 1849 was the year *The Essene Letter* was published in Germany. The 1840s had been a time of rationalist movements, which had resulted in the emergence of new religious bodies, such as the German Catholic Church and the Free Protestant congregations (*die freireligiöse Bewegung*, or colloquially, *Lichtfreunde*, "friends of light").[57] Religious freedom in Germany had been extended in 1847, and the February revolution of 1848 gave promises for continued liberal development. Liberalism in the 1840s also meant new religious ideas of a radical kind. The modern science of nature, as well as that of the Bible, seemed to necessitate a new kind of Christianity in which Jesus was seen as an ordinary human being and his teaching as a moral doctrine, governed by reason. A new Bible discovery with this content was an idea likely to arouse enthusiasm.[58]

The setting of *The Essene Letter* may be specified still more exactly. The German brotherhood, said to be the editors of the letter, was no doubt meant to be a Masonic lodge. The "German translator" emphasized several times in his introduction that it was the Freemasons who were the real descendants of the Essenes. The ritual used for initiating Jesus and John into the brotherhood has evident Masonic features; in it the brethren placed "their right hands upon their breasts, with the left hanging down at the side" (page 50), and "the trowel, emblematic of the labours of our Brotherhood, was put into their hands" (page 51).[59]

The combination of rationalism and romantic secrecy expressed in *The Essene Letter* fits perfectly the ideology of Masonic circles in Germany at this time. Later editors, also, have evidently had Masonic connections. The preface of the American edition of 1907 was written by a person with such interests, who also claimed that the original manuscript was in the hands of German Masons; this edition also has an appendix on "the Order of Essees" (sic), said to be a manuscript for Freemasons. The latest American version (from 1975) was published by a New York lodge with an undefinable Masonic affiliation.

The Essene Letter gave rise to a great deal of sensationalism from its very beginning, even if the important theological periodicals preferred to observe a contemptuous silence. The book had been written in order to appeal to the people, and it was in the newspapers and in booklets that the debate was carried on.

The Essene Letter also has a further history. In 1879 it became the cause of another apocryphal book in German, *The Fifth Gospel* or *The Original Gospel of the Essenes*. The originator was Friedrich Clemens (a pseudonym for Friedrich Clemens Gerke), who had belonged to the "freethinkers" since the 1840s, and who had pub-

lished a few books in a naturalist and rationalist spirit. He created
his new Gospel by mixing parts from the four biblical Gospels with
passages from *The Essene Letter,* molding them into a new syn-
thesis with the Luther Bible as a model. Unlike *The Essene Letter,*
his book is divided into chapters and verses in the traditional way.
The editor intended his new Gospel for use by congregations of
freethinkers (*freireligiöse Gemeinden*) but it does not seem to have
been a success and has now sunk into complete oblivion. As it was a
conscious composition, there is no story of an alleged discovery
involved.

Following its original publication, *The Essene Letter* was soon
translated into other languages. A French translation appeared in
1863 but without visible success. In Sweden it became far more
popular, with six editions so far, the two latest both published in
1977.[60]

The real impact of the letter, however, came through the
American editions, already mentioned. This occurred through the
Ahmadiyya movement, a branch of Islam, which claims that Jesus
survived the crucifixion, that he finally died in northern India and
was buried in Srinagar, the capital of Kashmir. We shall hear more
about this in a following chapter. *The Essene Letter* was translated
from English into Urdu in the beginning of this century, and thus
established a market in Pakistan and Kashmir. The American edition from 1907 is still being reprinted by the Ahmadiyya movement.
Its intensive use of the letter for its mission will secure the future
spread of this forgery.

But what about the real question: was Jesus an Essene or not?
This problem has been much debated since the Qumran discoveries
were made, and the present standpoint of most exegetes is that it
is not very likely that he ever belonged to the Essene brotherhood.
On the other hand, he may very well have had knowledge of it,
and he may have learned of its traditions, perhaps through John
the Baptist.[61] These questions will certainly continue to be discussed
in the future, but *The Essene Letter* will never have a true place
in this debate. It gives us no knowledge about realities during the
time of Jesus.

8

Pilate's Own Story

To Tiberius Caesar.

A young man appeared in Galilee and, in the name of God who sent him, preached a new law. At first I thought that his intention was to stir up a revolt among the people against the Romans. My suspicions were soon dispelled. Jesus of Nazareth spoke more as a friend of the Romans than as a friend of the Jews.

One day I observed a young man among a group of people, leaning against the trunk of a tree and speaking quietly to the crowd that surrounded him. They told me that he was Jesus. This was obvious because of the great difference between him and those around him. His fair hair and beard gave him a divine appearance. He was about thirty years old, and never before had I seen such a pleasant, kind face. What a vast difference there was between him, with his fair complexion, and those, wearing black beards, who were listening to him. As I did not want to disturb him, I went on my way, telling my secretary, however, to join the group and listen.

Later my secretary told me that he had never read in the works of the philosophers anything that could be compared to the teachings of Jesus, and that he was neither leading the people astray nor an agitator. That is why we decided to protect him. He was free to act, to talk, and to call a gathering of the people. This unlimited liberty provoked the Jews, who were indignant; it did not upset the poor but it irritated the rich and powerful. Later I wrote a letter to Jesus asking for an interview at the Forum. He came. When the Nazarene appeared I was taking my morning stroll, and, looking at him, I was transfixed. My feet seemed fettered with iron chains to the marble floor; I was trembling all over as a guilty person would, although he was calm. Without moving, I appraised this exceptional man for some time. There was nothing unpleasant about his appearance or character. In his presence I felt a profound respect for him. I told him that he had an infectious simplicity that set him above the present-day philosophers and masters. He made a deep impression on all of us, owing to his pleasant manner, simplicity, humility, and love. These, worthy sovereign, are the deeds that concern Jesus of Nazareth, and I have taken time to inform you in detail about this affair. My opinion is that a man who is capable of turning water into wine, who heals the sick, who resuscitates the dead and calms rough seas is not guilty of a criminal act. As others have said, we must admit that he is really the son of God.

Your obedient Servant,
Pontius Pilate

This letter—which has not the slightest ring of authenticity—has appeared in a fairly recent book by Andreas Faber-Kaiser, a European enthusiast for the Ahmadiyya Jesus legend.[62] According to Faber-Kaiser, this letter was written in A.D. 32; the original is preserved in the British Museum, and "it is possible to acquire copies of it at the Library of Congress in Washington." Perhaps this alleged letter has been printed in one form or another before and may be hidden somewhere in the said library, but it is by no means an ancient document. It is nothing but a condensed version of the earlier *Report of Pilate*, which had a notable success about 150 years ago, and which has reappeared several times since then.

Pontius Pilate is one of the enigmatic figures in the history of Jesus. His ambiguous behavior, seen in his dual role as both adversary and half-hearted defender of Jesus, calls for explanation. Not unexpectedly, Pilate has been a recurrent figure in literature and fiction. In early Christian times, there was already an apocryphal literature around the figure of Pilate, with interest centered around the conversation between Pilate and Jesus. The writings known collectively as the *Acts of Pilate* have no value as historic sources, but they were widely spread as a popular reading matter.[63] The most well-known book of this literary genre is *The Gospel of Nicodemus*, translated into many languages.

When Constantin Tischendorf made his famous discoveries in the Orient in the 1850s, he also found a number of unknown Acts of Pilate, which were printed then for the first time. Probably it was this success that inspired an American minister to publish an apocryphon of his own, *The Report of Pilate*. His name was W. D. Mahan, and he was a Presbyterian minister from Boonville, Missouri.

According to the Reverend Mahan, he had learned in 1856 that there was a Latin manuscript in the Vatican library with a report written by Pilate himself, and in 1859 he was given a translation of the text, delivered via several middlemen. The three persons he named — Henry C. Whydaman, Peter Freelinhusen, and C. C. Vantberger — have never been traced, in spite of the assertion that Freelinhusen was "chief guardian of the Vatican."

It was not until 1879 that Mahan published the report; the little book became such a success that a second edition was issued the next year.[64] At the same time it captured the interest of a certain William Overton Clough, who gave it a place in his edition of the so-called *Gesta Pilati*. This curious collection mainly consists of early Christian Acts of Pilate, taken from Alexander Walker's English translation of Tischendorf's text. The collection also includes obscure material such as *The Death Warrant of Jesus* (in the copperplate version) and *A Correct Transcription of Pilate's Court*, which is nothing but Mahan's *Report of Pilate*. Clough was also able to print parts of the report in Latin, which is said to be of a rather dubious kind. It was most remarkable that he had obtained the Latin text. Mahan only claimed to have a translation, and his middlemen had gone underground by then. There seems to be no doubt that the Latin fragments were fabricated by Clough.

The story relates Pilate's agony during the trial of Jesus. His wife implores him to acquit Jesus, but he does not have sufficient Roman troops to resist those led by the Jewish priests and elders and yields to their wishes. The expected reinforcement of 2,000 soldiers does not arrive until the evening after the execution, to the grief of Pilate, who sees himself as the victim of a cruel destiny.

It is a romantic story with theatrical effects, and it is strange that this typical product by a nineteenth-century novelist may have been mistaken for a real writing in Pilate's own hand. As Goodspeed has shown, Mahan unabashedly plagiarized an existing story, and I am happy to have identified the original author: it was the French dramatician Joseph Méry (1798–1867), who wrote a number of short stories in his youth.[65] The original story, *Ponce Pilate à Vienne*, was published in the *Revue de Paris* in 1837; a comparison with Mahan's "manuscript" reveals a literal agreement in every detail, except where the text has been distorted by mistranslations or misreadings. In the original version, Pilate tells his story to his friend Fabius Albinus during a visit to his home in Vienne. As we have seen, Vienne was believed of old to be the place were Pilate died and was buried. This framework for the story was cut away by Mahan in order to make more believable, if only slightly so, his claim that his story had been found in an ancient manuscript.

The idea to transform Méry's story into an apocryphal manuscript probably came from the story itself. Méry wrote in his introduction that he had been inspired by an old Latin manuscript which he had recently read. It might have been one of the ancient Acts of Pilate that Méry had obtained; moreover, he never claimed that the plot of the story could be found in the manuscript he had read. But so it has soon been understood. The earliest translations of this popular story—to Italian and Spanish—still indicate Méry as the author, but in 1842 an American translation was published, in which the story was said to have been taken from an old Latin manuscript found in Vienne. This translation, *Pontius Pilate's Account of the Condemnation of Jesus Christ and his own Mental Sufferings*, is possibly the book where Mahan found the story. It is also possible that he believed in the assertion that it had been taken from an ancient document, even if he later—in a way characteristic for him—preferred to appear himself as its discoverer. Goodspeed reports a fantastic course of events regarding how the story was later translated into Arabic by an Orthodox bishop, Jerasimus Jared, and from there into English, and that it then found a new life as an apocryphon in Australia. Méry could hardly have imagined that his little story would be such a world-wide success.

I am more doubtful about Goodspeed's opinion that Méry's story might have inspired Anatole France to write his ironical story *The Procurator of Judaea*.[66] The only similarity is that Pilate tells an old friend about his life, and France may well have got this idea without having read Méry's story. But there might be something here that I have not seen.

Plagiarizing fiction and pretending that the plagiarism was an ancient document proved to be a profitable business. Intoxicated with the success of the *Report of Pilate*, Mahan began to make new and sensational discoveries. In 1884 he was able to publish no fewer than twelve similar documents under the magnificent title *The Archaeological and the Historical Writings of the Sanhedrin and Talmuds of the Jews, Translated from the Ancient Parchments and Scrolls at Constantinople and the Vatican at Rome*. This volume has been reprinted several times, often with the title *The Archko Volume* or *Archko Library*.[67]

Mahan made a show of having been to Rome and Constantinople, and pretended to have found some of the published writings in the library of the Hagia Sophia. Observant readers, however, could soon realize that great parts of the contents and many literal wordings had been taken from Lew Wallace's popular novel *Ben-Hur* (1880). The most amusing detail in Goodspeed's account is how a reader began to wonder about the strange word *anuman*, which appeared to be something worshipped by the Egyptians. A comparison with *Ben-Hur* showed that Mahan had been careless with his reading; he had happened to omit one line in the novel, and *anuman* proved to be a most illegitimate crossbreed of Anu-bis and Ahri-man!

Mahan had to answer for his miserable fraud before the presbytery of Lebanon. Lew Wallace could testify that Mahan never had been to Constantinople, still less in the library of the Hagia Sophia. Wallace himself had just paid a visit to Istanbul, and in his position of an American general, he had had no difficulties in getting all relevant information from the American and Turkish authorities.

Mahan was sentenced to a year's suspension and had to do penance for his foolishness, yet there was nothing to prevent new editions of his forgeries. Goodspeed tells us that *The Archko Volume* was used for readings in broadcasting programs from Davenport, Iowa, in 1926, but there certainly are signs of a later survival in Faber-Kaiser's abbreviated version.[68]

In a Swedish publication with a somewhat fascist tendency, I recently saw a reference to the passage quoted at the beginning of this chapter. The "fair complexion" of Jesus was taken as an indication that he was not Jewish but of Aryan origin. An interesting point is that the author of the article in question referred to Professors McIntosh and Twyman, who were said to have vouched for the authenticity of the document in 1935 and 1976. These two persons are well known from the history of *The Archko Volume*, for they were precisely the authorities to whom Mahan referred in 1884. Like so many of Mahan's references, they were never to be found in the real world; they surely seem to have been long-lived, however, for in 1976, when they made their latest statement, both must have been far more than a hundred years old. The author of the Swedish article is, unfortunately, unable to tell me where he had found this information; perhaps the reader may be more fortunate.

The Reverend Mahan himself does not seem to have had any ideological basis for his fraud. No heretical doctrines or new ideas are involved in his publications, which generally follow his prototypes in a most unimaginative way. Neither did he possess any literary genius; he took everything from earlier authors, often with disastrous results — as when the "drooping lids" of the Virgin Mary became "dropping" ones! The only visible urge behind his efforts was the lust to arouse sensation, yet he sometimes excused himself with the argument that his activity was both innocuous and helpful. "You are bound to admit," he wrote in a letter, "that the items in the book cant [sic] do any harm even if it were faulce [sic], but will cause many to read and reflect that otherwise would not."

9

Jesus in India

1. In the course of his fourteenth year, young Issa, blessed by God, journeyed beyond the Sindh and settled among the Aryas in the beloved country of God.

2. The fame of his name spread along the Northern Sindh. When he passed through the country of the five rivers and the Radjipoutan, the worshipers of the God Djaïne begged him to remain in their midst.

3. But he left the misguided admirers of Djaïne and visited Juggernaut, in the province of Orsis, where the remains of Viassa-Krishna rest, and where he received a joyous welcome from the white priests of Brahma.

4. They taught him to read and understand the Vedas, to heal by prayer, to teach and explain the Holy Scripture, to cast out evil spirits from the body of man and give him back human semblance.

5. He spent six years in Juggernaut, Rajegriha, Benares, and the other holy cities; all loved him, for Issa lived in peace with the Vaisyas and the Soudras, to whom he taught the Holy Scripture.

6. But the Brahmans and the Kshatriyas declared that the Great Para-Brahma forbade them to approach those whom he had created from his entrails and from his feet.

7. That the Vaisyas were authorized to listen only to the reading of the Vedas, and that never save on feast days.

8. That the Soudras were not only forbidden to attend the reading of the Vedas, but to gaze upon them even; for their condition was to perpetually serve and act as slaves to the Brahmans, the Kshatriyas, and even to the Vaisyas.

9. "Death alone can free them from servitude," said Para-Brahma. "Leave them, therefore, and worship with us the gods who will show their anger against you if you disobey them."

10. But Issa would not heed them; and going to the Soudras, preached against the Brahmans and the Kshatriyas.

11. He strongly denounced the men who robbed their fellow-beings of their rights as men, saying: "God the Father establishes no difference between his children, who are all equally dear to him."

*The Unknown Life of
Jesus Christ*, ch. 5

We now arrive at the best-known Gospel forgery of modern times. Its entire history has been extensively explored by Goodspeed; the reader may also profit from rereading the original documents. The book aroused a sensation and achieved an explosive spread, only to be disclosed as a forgery in a short time and to sink back into oblivion. The book has also had a more recent history, however, in which the story has been revived and has continued to fascinate unto this day. This latest development has been subsequent to the last edition of Goodspeed's book and may be told here instead.

But let us take the whole story from the beginning. In 1894, the Russian war correspondent Nicolas Notovitch published a travel book in French, which soon became the topic of the day.[69] Its title was *The Unknown Life of Jesus Christ (La vie inconnue de Jésus-Christ)*, and referred to a sensational discovery that Notovitch pretended to have made. During travels in India and Kashmir in 1887 (possibly as a Russian spy, for this was the time of Rudyard Kipling's *Kim*), he heard Tibetan lamas tell stories about the prophet Issa, who was said to be greatly honored among the Tibetans, and he got the idea that this prophet might in fact be none but Jesus. (So far the story may be true, for Issa is the Tibetan form of the name of Jesus.)

Notovitch traveled to Leh, the capital of the district of Ladakh on the border between India and Tibet, and near there he went to the monastery of Hemis, still a center of Tibetan Buddhism. He was told that the monastery was in the possession of scrolls inscribed with the *Life of Saint Issa;* he dared not ask to see them at that stage but told the monks that he would return later. But—by a stroke of good or bad luck, as you prefer—he fell from his horse just a few days later and broke his leg, and so he was carried back to the monastery to be nursed.

While he was convalescing, attended only by a youth who kept a prayer wheel in motion, he found that the chance had come to see the extraordinary book about Issa and to have it translated. He persuaded the abbot to read to him from the book, which appeared to be in Tibetan in two large bound volumes. As he did not understand the language, he had it all translated by an interpreter. For many nights, he went without sleep to order and remodel what he

58

had heard. According to Notovitch, the printed text was thus orally translated by an interpreter and also reworked afterwards.[70]

It was here that Notovitch obtained confirmation that Saint Issa was none other than Jesus himself, and that he heard ancient legends about Jesus forgotten in the West. He learned that Jesus had wandered to India and to Tibet as a young man before he began his work in Palestine. According to the story, Jesus had met Jains, Brahmins, and Buddhists; he had learned Pali and had studied the sacred writings of the Buddhists until he returned again to the West. On his way back, Jesus preached to the Zoroastrians in Persia, and then he began his work in Palestine. Here the story quickly turns to the passion and suffering of Christ in a fairly well-known form and tells us, like the canonical Gospels, that the tomb was found empty on the third day.

According to Notovitch, the abbot had declared that the manuscripts were translations to Tibetan from Pali texts, preserved in Lhasa. Actually, Pali, which is the sacred language of Theravada Buddhism, has never been used in Tibet, and the Tibetan translations have usually been done from Sanskrit or from Chinese.

Notovitch's story caused a sensation in the West. In one year eight editions were published in French; three American translations and an English one followed immediately, and the book was also translated into several other languages.

The style and content of the book are indicated in the passage quoted in the beginning of this chapter.[71] Some of the oddities can also be found in the original French edition. In particular, the reference to "the god Djaïne" reveals a considerable lack of knowledge about Indian religions. The Jains, or Jainas, do not believe in any god at all, but in certain *jinas* ("conquerors"), who are enlightened spiritual leaders. The *a* in *Jain* comes from the phonetic law that makes the worshipers of Shiva into *Shaivas* and the worshipers of Vishnu into *Vaishnavas.*

The fame of Notovitch lasted for a short time, then the criticism began. It was opened by no less than Professor Max Müller of Oxford, who was the greatest Indologist of the West, and the editor of the large collection of texts from the Orient, named *The Sacred Books of the East.*

Müller went into his attack in an article in *The Nineteenth Century*.[71] He began by stating how common it was to locate mysteries to Tibet. He probably had Madame Blavatsky and her mahatmas in mind, for this was just the time when her correspondence through the air with hidden masters in Himalaya was being reported in the world press. Müller also pointed out that Hemis was not such an unknown place as Notovitch had described it, but a well-known monastery, which was often visited by occidentals.

Concerning the alleged writing, Müller declared that such an old document — from the first century A.D. according to Notovitch — would undoubtedly have been included in those great catalogues, known as the Kanjur and Tanjur, in which all Tibetan literature has been listed. The Kanjur contains the more specifically Buddhist literature. If the book existed, it would rather be included in the Tanjur, and Notovitch's informants would have been able to point out where it could be found.

Müller also rejected the story about the origin of the book. Jewish merchants from Palestine were said to have carried accounts of Jesus to India after his death, and from their description the Indians had later recognized young Issa, who had once studied Buddhist writings there. This would require two conditions, which are both quite unlikely: that among the masses of India, the Jews had found the exact persons involved, and that these individuals understood that the Jews were talking about the same person they knew. Müller preferred not to accuse Notovitch of fraud, however, but allowed for the possibility that he had been cheated by the monks at Hemis.

Max Müller's article said that missionaries and British officers had been asked about the doings of Notovitch, but that they had not seen any Russian traveler. More precise information was given in a letter from an English woman who had looked into the matter; it came in time to be printed as an appendix to the article. The woman had visited Hemis and had made inquiries, and it appeared that no Russian had visited the monastery for a long time. No one had been taken there with a broken leg for the last years, and there was no trace of *Saint Issa's Life*.

The final verdict on Notovitch's story was passed two years later in a second article in *The Nineteenth Century*, this time by Professor J. Archibald Douglas of Agra.[72] He had used his three months' vacation from the local university to retrace Notovitch's journey through the valley of the Sindh, where he found no sign of those panthers and tigers which Notovitch had so vividly described. Douglas also went to Leh and Hemis. The main part of his article consists of an interview with the abbot of the monastery, held with the retired postmaster of Leh serving as interpreter.

With the help of the interpreter, Douglas read Notovitch's book to the abbot, who listened with increasing astonishment to all that he had allegedly said to Notovitch seven or eight years earlier. During the interview, he declared that he had been the abbot for fifteen years, and that no European with an injured leg had been seen in the monastery during this time. He further declared that he had been a lama for forty-two years, and that he was well acquainted with Buddhist literature, but that he had never heard of any book or manuscript in which the name Issa was mentioned. He also expressed his firm belief that no such book existed. According to Notovitch, the abbot had made statements about the religions of the ancient Egyptians, the Assyrians, and the people of Israel, but the lama emphatically declared that he did not know anything about these peoples or their religions. Finally, he wondered if in Europe there existed no means of punishing a person who told such untruths as Notovitch had. The interview was written down and witnessed by the abbot, Douglas, and the interpreter, and was sealed with the official seal of the abbot.

In a later paragraph, Max Müller apologized to the lamas of Hemis for his earlier hint that they might have taken Notovitch in. It had become entirely clear who the real cheat was.

Before the final blow fell in 1896, Notovitch had begun to retreat from his position. In the preface of the 1895 edition, he admitted that there was no manuscript about Issa but now said that the story had been gathered from various books in the monastery. This statement was of no great help to him, however, since it was now known that he had never been in the monastery at all. Notovitch gave up the role of religious discoverer and returned to his war correspondence. The end of his life was spent mostly in obscurity.

Unlike most Gospel forgers, Notovitch had no ideological motive for writing his account of the life of Jesus. His primary aim was to arouse sensation through a more intelligent version of Mahan's work, and this contributes to the vagueness of the alleged writing. But Notovitch had the good luck to publish his book during the heyday of romanticism about India. In 1877, Queen Victoria had been crowned Empress of India, Max Müller and his fellow workers were translating the religious legacy of India into English, Madame Blavatsky corresponded with her mahatmas,[73] and the idea that Christianity might have a Buddhist origin was also abroad.[74] Notovitch published his book just at the right moment, and thus experienced a short-lived fame as a discoverer.

The reader may now wonder whether Notovitch had been to the Orient at all. He certainly had, as Douglas could report. Notovitch had even been to Leh and had been treated, not for a broken leg, but for a toothache at the Moravian mission station, and oddly enough by a missionary named Karl Marx. A friend of mine who has visited Leh has told me that such a treatment can hardly have been a pleasure; this gives a grim satisfaction, when all the later confusion caused by Notovitch is taken into consideration.

The story proved to be too good to be forgotten forever. After some time it came back, often without any mention of Notovitch's name or of the disclosure of the fraud. In 1926, the book came out in a new edition in New York; once more, it was observed in the press throughout the world, for the events at the turn of the century had now sunk into pleasant oblivion. Before that Notovitch had certainly inspired others to write similar works. Neither Ouseley's *Gospel of the Holy Twelve* nor Dowling's *Aquarian Gospel* would have been written without Notovitch as a source of inspiration.

Nor has the disclosure of Notovitch's deception discouraged others from following his path to Hemis in order to seek the desired manuscripts.[75] Professor Nicholas Roerich, painter and amateur archaeologist, traveled in Ladakh in the 1920s and believed that he had found traces of *The Life of Saint Issa*. Unfortunately, his examples from living folk traditions lend no added reliability, for the first part of his account is taken literally from Notovitch's *Life of Saint Issa*, chapters 5–13 (only extracts but with all the verses in the right order). It is followed by "another version" (pages 93–94), taken from chapter 16 of Dowling's *Aquarian Gospel*. There is a vague possibility that visiting enthusiasts from Europe had already spread these stories to Ladakh, and that they had taken root in popular belief. But Roerich's literal quotations rather suggest that he inserted them only because he found them attractive. He was of a romantic nature and seems not to have taken a great interest in more tangible facts.

The legend about Jesus' sojourn in India is today mostly cherished by the Ahmadiyya movement,[76] which has already been mentioned in connection with *The Essene Letter*. This movement, which is rejected by orthodox Islam, and which has a precarious existence in Islamic countries, has had a considerable following in the West. The two branches of the movement (with centers in Lahore and in Rabwah) each have a mosque in London, and both branches have issued a great number of publications.[77]

An important doctrine to Ahmadiyya is that Jesus never died on the cross but that he survived and later fled to Kashmir, where he died at a great age and was buried in Srinagar. The founder of Ahmadiyya, Hazrat Mirza Ghulam Ahmad from Qadiyan (1839?–1908), is believed by his followers to have been the promised Messiah and Mahdi, and he thus takes a position not unlike that of Jesus in Christianity. It is, therefore, in the interest of the movement to declare Jesus a figure from the past without real relevance to the present. Members of the movement are, therefore, unable to follow the Islamic doctrine that Jesus was taken up alive into heaven (cf p. 14). They believe instead that he died here on earth and was buried here. Ahmad himself has uttered this by divine inspiration, and he has also pointed out the site of the tomb.

The Ahmadiyya legend is generally supported by references to diverse Oriental sources, which are said to confirm the story, but which in fact do not carry any weight at all. There are also references to earlier legends, which we have already encountered. *The Gospel of Barnabas* is quoted by Ahmad as evidence that Jesus did not die on the cross, while the story about the Ascension in the same Gospel is certainly not mentioned.[78] *The Gospel of Barnabas* had not yet been published in its entirety during Ahmad's lifetime, and it is possible that Ahmad was not very well informed about its complete contents. It is quite possible that he had also heard about *The Essene Letter*, which was translated into English towards the end of the nineteenth century, and which may have inspired his idea that Jesus was just apparently dead. Ahmad knew of Notovitch's book and mentioned it in *Jesus in India* without really understanding its character. In later Ahmadiyya literature, both *The Essene Letter* and *The Life of Saint Issa* are quoted as authentic documents about Jesus.

But Ahmad's legend is not identical with that of Notovitch.[79] *The Life of Saint Issa* describes the life of Jesus in India before his work in Palestine. According to Ahmad, it was not until his escape from the cross that Jesus started his journey to the East. Only later Ahmadiyya writers have combined the two stories, letting Jesus visit India twice. In spite of the differences between Ahmad and Notovitch, it is not impossible that the latter inspired Ahmad to the idea that Jesus spent a part of his life in India.

It is, therefore, quite consistent that some of Ahmad's disciples and supporters have tried to obtain the documents that Notovitch told of. A Professor F. M. Hassnain[80] in Srinagar has told the press that he intends to have the documents made accessible in Hemis; his colleague Aziz Kashmiri has evidently been there on the same errand and is seen in a group picture with the Abbot of Hemis and several Indian journalists. It is ironic that the venerable monastery of Hemis, so rich in traditions, has won its universal fame through a book that it does not seem ever to have possessed!

In this context I cannot refrain from telling about some Jesus apocrypha from still more distant areas. In 1935, somebody in Japan discovered a document telling that Jesus had spent his youth on the island of Honshu, and that he returned there later in his life.[81] According to the story, it was not Jesus who was crucified but his brother Isukiri, and Jesus carried the latter's ears and hair on his wanderings through Siberia. He subsequently landed in Hachinoe, Aomori, and settled in Herai (today called Shingo), where he married and had three daughters. He died at the age of 106 and was laid in a burial mound in Herai; the relics of his brother were buried in a neighboring mound. The discoverer of these sensational matters, Mr. Hiromaro Takeuchi of Isohara in Ibaraki prefecture, set out for Herai to make inquiries; shortly afterwards some writings were discovered, which were said to have been written by Jesus himself, and to have been handed down from generation to genera-

tion. The inhabitants of Herai-Shingo take the whole matter seriously and celebrate Jesus yearly on the tenth of June—why just on that
day is not clear. The background of this curious story is as unknown
to me as to the reader. James Hall Roberts had perhaps heard of
it, for in his novel *The Q Document* he tells about a forged
autograph of Jesus found in Japan.

10

A Gospel for Vegetarians

1. When Jesus knew how the Pharisees had murmured and complained because he made and baptized more disciples than John, he left Judea, and departed again into Galilee.

2. And Jesus came to a certain Tree and abode beneath it many days. And there came Mary Magdalene and other women and ministered unto him of their substance, and he taught daily all that came unto him.

3. And the birds gathered around him, and welcomed him with their song, and other living creatures came unto his feet, and he fed them, and they ate out of his hands.

4. And when he departed he blessed the women who shewed love unto him, and turning to the fig tree, he blessed it also, saying, Thou hast given me shelter and shade from the burning heat, and withal thou hast given me food also.

5. Blessed be thou, increase and be fruitful, and let all who come to thee, find rest and shade and food, and let the birds of the air rejoice in thy branches.

6. And behold the tree grew and flourished exceedingly, and its branches took root downward, and sent shoots upward and it spread mightily, so that no tree was like unto it for its size and its beauty, and the abundance and goodness of its fruit.

7. And as Jesus entered into a certain village he saw a young cat which had none to care for her, and she was hungry and cried unto him, and he took her up, and put her inside his garment, and she lay in his bosom.

8. And when he came into the village he set food and drink before the cat, and she ate and drank, and showed thanks unto him. And he gave her unto one of his disciples, who was a widow, whose name was Lorenza, and she took care of her.

9. And some of the people said, This man careth for all creatures, are they his brothers and sisters that he should love them? And he said unto them, Verily these are your fellow creatures of the great Household of God, yea, they are your brethren and sisters, having the same breath of life in the Eternal.

10. And whosoever careth for one of the least of these, and giveth

it to eat and drink in its need, the same doeth it unto me, and whoso willingly suffereth one of these to be in want, and defendeth it not when evilly entreated, suffereth the evil as done unto me, for as ye have done in this life, so shall it be done unto you in the life to come.

The Gospel of the Holy Twelve, ch. 34

A friendly Jesus, who blesses and protects both plants and animals, and to whom birds and creeping things gather in a natural way—is this not the way that many of us want to think of him? Many have been attracted by the portrait of Jesus in The Gospel of the Holy Twelve, and have suggested that its ideals and ethics are higher than those of the canonical Gospels.[83] In England, where this book originated, it has come out in six or seven editions, the latest in 1972. Probably it has had an even greater success in Germany and in Sweden, where it has become a Bible of the health-food movement. The second Swedish edition, from 1976, is often seen on display in health food shops.

This writing is claimed to be an original Aramaic Gospel, older and more authentic than those of our New Testament. It is said to have been preserved in a Tibetan monastery, until it came into the care of an English clergyman, the Reverend G. J. R. Ouseley, who published it at the turn of the century. The German and Swedish editors declare that Mr. Ouseley found it in Tibet in 1881, but there is nothing to indicate that he had ever traveled in the Orient. The English edition from 1972 tells another story. Here the Gospel is said to have been written by St. John during his imprisonment in Rome and given page by page to a disciple. Later the "scroll" (which obviously had pages!) was taken by the disciple to a Tibetan monastery. There it was found in the 1870s by a Franciscan friar named Placidus, whom we will meet later in another context. On his way home, he translated parts of the Gospel into Latin, and in Rome he read it to an assembly of cardinals. They soon realized that this was an uncensured version of the Gospel, and therefore hid it away in the Vatican archives.

This writing claims that the canonical Gospels once contained teachings of Jesus "about the love and care for animals and about abstaining from eating flesh-foods," but these parts of the Gospels were allegedly suppressed at the Council of Nicaea in A.D. 325. Every student of the New Testament and of the history of the early church should know immediately how baseless these claims are. The canons of Nicaea have been preserved, and they have nothing to say about the text of the New Testament. Moreover, we possess today a number of papyri from the second and third centuries which show us clearly that the text did not go through any drastic changes in the fourth century.

Chapter 34 of *The Gospel of the Holy Twelve*, which has been quoted here in full, gives a clear impression of the general style and content of the book, even if the aspects of vegetarianism and health food are lacking just here. Throughout, the book is written in a kind of smoothed "biblical style," combining traits from the four Evangelists and other New Testament writers. The disposition is the same as in Matthew and Luke. The story begins with the childhood of Jesus and leads on to the resurrection and a kind of ascension story. Most of the book tells us about wanderings of Jesus; he encounters various people and, perhaps more important, animals, and he holds long discourses with his disciples. The style is at times somewhat sentimental. Flowers spring up in the footsteps of Jesus, he speaks the language of birds and of beasts, and a lion lies down innocuously at his feet.

Other features are well known from similar literature. As in *The Aquarian Gospel*, Jesus travels in his youth to Assyria and India, to Persia and Chaldaea (6:13); as in *The Essene Letter*, he learns "the healing powers of trees, and of herbs, and of flowers" (6:12); as in *The Gospel of Peace*, he preaches a polarity between fatherhood and motherhood, but here these are not represented by two powers but by a single divine Father-Mother (Abba-Amma 19:1, 76:11).[84] This last trait may appeal to those who have taken issue with the onesidedly masculine metaphors for God in the Bible. As in so many modern apocrypha, Mary Magdalene is described as the partner of Jesus (66:9). Towards the end of the Gospel (96:23), the apostles confess their belief in reincarnation, which is never mentioned in our New Testament.

The real reason for the success of this Gospel is its propaganda for vegetarian food. Both Jesus and John the Baptist reject bloody sacrifices, hunting, and flesh-eating. Instead, Jesus preaches a diet of fruit and of herbs:

> And, for thy living, behold the fields yielding their increase, and the fruit-bearing trees and the herbs: what needest thou more than these which honest work of thy hands will not give thee? Woe to the strong who misuse their strength. Woe to the crafty who hurt the creatures of God. Woe to the hunters, for they shall be hunted [14:7].

Accordingly, Jesus feeds the multitude with five melons (48:1-4); he celebrates Passover without a lamb (75:6-9); and he preaches a diet of fruits and of herbs.

However attractive this may seem to some readers, the question remains what kind of book it is, whether it has an ancient origin and conveys some authentic traditions about Jesus, or whether it is just a modern imitation. Critical study of the content will soon reveal dubious features.

The Swedish editor points out, quite unsuspectingly, how much more rich in detail this "original Gospel" is in comparison with the canonical Gospels, and also how many difficult and objectionable passages are given a simple and natural explanation. She herself reveals the reason for doubting its authenticity, for a richness in details and a lack of difficulties are just signs that it is an extended and smoothed version of the Gospel story. A general principle when ancient documents are compared is that the shortest and the most difficult reading has to be preferred.[85]

The Gospel of the Holy Twelve is purported to be older than the four canonical Gospels of our Bible. It, therefore, seems strange that passages from all the four Gospels appear here. The Magi occur in Matthew, the birth of John the Baptist in Luke, the introduction in John. The book gives rather the impression of having been composed by joining parts of the Gospels and other biblical literature. There are several quotations from Saint Paul, such as 1 Corinthians 13:1 and 15:22 in sections 69:2 and 94:7 respectively. Section 52:9 contains a version of an apocryphal Jesus saying, widely spread in the early Church.[86]

On the other hand, is it this older Gospel that is quoted by the four Evangelists and by Paul? Such a theory does not work, for the Evangelists as well as Paul have typical stylistic features by which we recognize them, and it is very easy to see which one is the primary source. In this case, the New Testament writers were certainly the first on the spot.

The "original Gospel" further reveals itself through use of certain words and expressions that evidently belong to a much later time. Such a word is *trinity* (19:3, 96:18), which is lacking in the New Testament and did not appear until the end of the second century.[87] Still more curious is what is written in 96:20 about "the Sevenfold Spirit of God, the Life-Giver: Who proceedeth from the holy Twain." The idea that the Spirit is sevenfold comes from Isaiah 11:2 and Revelation 1:4f, but the expression is from a far later time. When the Spirit is called "Life-Giver" and is said to "proceed," this shows that the author knew the Nicene Creed (in its revised form from Constantinople 381), in which the third article confesses "the Holy Spirit, the Lord and giver of life, who proceeds from the Father." Furthermore, when it is said that the Spirit "proceedeth from the Holy Twain," this shows that the author was influenced by the so-called *filioque,* the concept that the Holy Spirit proceeds from the Father and the Son, although this has been reinterpreted as referring to the "Father-Mother." The *filioque* is a Western insertion into the creed which cannot be traced before the time of Charlemagne.[88] The book cannot, therefore, be older than from the time around 800. As we shall see, it is in fact more than a thousand years younger.

The fauna described in this book is not quite that of the Bible. We here find a cat, which is rescued by Jesus (ch.34), rabbits (28:1) and an ape, mentioned by Jesus (28:2). None of these animals are mentioned in the Bible. Even if these species existed in Palestine, it would be interesting to know the words for them in the alleged original Aramaic text. Even more dubious is the story (in 21:1–6) of a man who used a horse for carrying a burden, for in Palestine only donkeys were used for that purpose. The man who trained dogs to hunt (ch.14) definitely belongs to the England of the nineteenth century, where the book, as we shall see, has its roots. All these zoological oddities together give an impression of dubious authenticity.

The end of the Gospel shows an interest in liturgical forms that more often belong to later times. That incense was used outside the temple cult may be acceptable, but the wedding ceremony (92:3) has been taken from the later rites of the Eastern churches.[89] The account of Jesus in which "casting a fragment of the Bread into the Cup, he blessed the holy Union" (76:22), shows that the author was familiar with the rite of the Roman mass known as *commixtio*.[90]

It should now be clear to most readers that we are dealing not with an unknown Gospel from early Christian times, but with a modern and rather clumsily made forgery. There is virtually nothing at all in this "Gospel" that has the slightest ring of authenticity. We are also fairly well informed about its origin.

The man behind *The Gospel of the Holy Twelve* was an Anglican clergyman, the Reverend Gideon Jasper Richard Ouseley (1835–1906).[91] His ecclesiastical career in Victorian Britain passed almost entirely unnoticed, but there are some fragments of information that may be combined into some kind of biographical sketch. He was born in Lisbon, the younger son of Sir Ralph Ouseley, and was brought to Ireland in 1842 on his father's death. He graduated at Trinity College in Dublin in 1858, and was ordained a clergyman of the Established Church in 1860 by the Bishop of Down and Connor. In 1861 he became curate of Warrenpoint, County Down, and probably also had other curacies in the 1860s. About 1870 he left the Anglican Church and was received as a priest of the Catholic Apostolic (Irvingite) Church. At that time he had already developed strongly vegetarian ideals. He wrote about ten books on vegetarianism and on occult matters.[92] He also founded a number of societies with theosophical and vegetarian goals, such as the Order of the At-one-ment and United Templars Society. These societies are otherwise completely unknown to us; it is possible that they consisted of only Ouseley and perhaps a few friends.

In 1882 he was living in London, but he moved to Brighton in the following year and stayed there until his death. There is a gap in our knowledge from 1872 to 1882, including also the year 1881, when he— according to some rumors— should have found the manuscript in Tibet. But, as we shall see, Ouseley never claimed to have been in Tibet, and there is no reason to investigate that matter more deeply. It was probably during this period that he left the Catholic

Apostolic Church, which did not agree with his vegetarian puritanism. Instead, he became deeply involved in the "Hermetic" movement of Anna Kingsford and Edward Maitland,[93] in which antivivisectionism and animal welfare were combined with a kind of theosophy, slightly different from the contemporary teaching of Madame Blavatsky. In Maitland's biography of Anna Kingsford, Ouseley appears (identified by the initials "I. O.") as "a priest deeply devoted to things mystical" and as an admirer of Kingsford's and Maitland's book *The Perfect Way*.[94] As we shall see, the impact of these two was greater than this little notice might give us a reason to suppose.

In a letter dated April 14, 1897, Ouseley says that he had received a spiritualist message "under the most trustworthy conditions" from the Swedish eighteenth-century mystic Emanuel Swedenborg, that Edward Maitland, who had died two weeks earlier, was "in the unseen already."[95] It was not long before he had direct communication with him. In the original edition of *The Gospel of the Holy Twelve*, Ouseley clearly states that he got its text by spiritualist communications from Swedenborg, Anna Kingsford, Edward Maitland, and the Franciscan friar Placidus, whom we met in the beginning of this chapter.[96] Ouseley and perhaps some assistant (he speaks of "editors") received it from the spiritual world in the form of many short messages.

The foreword of the 1972 edition provides more details about how the Gospel was transmitted through "dreams and visions of the night." Ouseley used to have visions of a lectern with manuscripts, and as it revolved, he read them during the night. In the morning, when his eyes were sore from the reading, he wrote down from memory what he had seen. The procedure is strongly reminiscent of the tale told about a similar writing, *The Aquarian Gospel*, which was also given to the editor in the hours of the night. We shall meet this writing in the next chapter.

If the book was revealed to Ouseley in this way, how can it be a translation from the Aramaic, and how is it related to the alleged manuscript in a Tibetan monastery or in Rome? How this is possible is clearly told in the original foreword. It was the spirits who made the translation and who gave Ouseley the text in English.

Nothing is said about a visit by Ouseley to Tibet, or that he had ever seen the original manuscript. This was quite unnecessary, when he had such effective communications of a spiritual kind. As in the case of *The Book of Mormon*, the alleged manuscript only served as justification of a writing that had evidently been transmitted by personal inspiration. Probably, Notovitch's book from 1894 and Madame Blavatsky's *The Secret Doctrine* from 1888 had given Ouseley the idea of telling the story about the manuscript. The foreword also makes it clear how the extensive parts from the four Gospels were placed into the text. The spirits had given Ouseley detailed instructions about how to insert quotations from the Authorized Version.

The spiritualist origin of the writing has been more or less consciously hidden by the German and Swedish editors to give the impression that Ouseley found a real Aramaic manuscript in Tibet. The real situation, however, was understood by Annie Besant, the leader of the Adyar Theosophists after the death of Madame Blavatsky.[97] In a fairly acid review entitled "A Strange Book," she makes it clear how the book came into existence, and also points out that it contains nothing to justify a claim of a special inspiration, as it is obviously "a collection from many sources." As for the contents, she states that it "does not rise above a rather low level of mediocrity, wherever there is anything which is not a quotation from familiar sources." There is no reason to disagree with this judgment, harsh as it may seem.

Let us summarize the entire matter: *The Gospel of the Holy Twelve*, also known as *The Gospel of the Perfect Life*, certainly is not a document from early Christianity, and there is no reason to suppose the existence of an Aramaic original or a manuscript in Tibet or Rome. It was compiled by G. J. R. Ouseley at the turn of the century in the interests of vegetarianism and animal welfare. A further question may be whether these ideals might in some way justify or at least excuse its composer. It is not my task to judge the morality of the Reverend Ouseley, or to decide whether he really believed that his editorial work was controlled by higher spirits. His openness about the procedure certainly speaks in his favor. Today his book has probably few readers in the English-speaking

73

world and is conspicuously missing in Goodspeed's otherwise so comprehensive work. Its popularity today is among health-food circles on the European continent. It is a pious wish that the health food movement — well known for its disapproval of synthetic products — might drop this unnecessary book from further publication.

11

A Gospel for the New Age

1. A caravan of merchantmen was journeying through the Kashmar vale as Jesus passed that way, and they were going to Lahore, a city of the Hand, the five-stream land.

2. The merchantmen had heard the prophet speak, had seen his mighty works in Leh, and they were glad to see him once again.

3. And when they knew that he was going to Lahore and then across the Sind, through Persia and the farther West, and that he had no beast on which to ride,

4. They freely gave to him a noble bactrian beast,well saddled and equipped, and Jesus journeyed with the caravan.

5. And when he reached Lahore, Ajainin and some other Brahmic priests received him with delight.

6. Ajainin was the priest who came to Jesus in the night time in Benares many months before, and heard his words of truth.

7. And Jesus was Ajainin's guest; he taught Ajainin many things; revealed to him the secrets of the healing art.

8. He taught him how he could control the spirits of the air, the fire, the water and the earth; and he explained to him the secret doctrine of forgiveness, and the blotting out of sins.

9. One day Ajainin sat with Jesus in the temple porch; a band of wandering singers and musicians paused before the court to sing and play.

10. Their music was most rich and delicate, and Jesus said, Among the high-breed people of the land we hear no sweeter music than that these uncouth children of the wilderness bring here to us.

11. From whence this talent and this power? In one short life they surely could not gain such grace of voice, such harmony, such knowledge of the laws of harmony and tone.

12. Men call them prodigies. There are no prodigies. All things result from natural law.

13. These people are not young. A thousand years would not suffice to give them such divine expressiveness, and such purity of voice and touch.

14. Ten thousand years ago these people mastered harmony. In days of old they trod the busy thoroughfares of life, and caught the melody of birds, and played on harps of perfect form.

15. And they have come again to learn still other lessons from the varied notes of manifests.

16. These wandering people form a part of heaven's orchestra, and in the land of perfect things the very angels will delight to hear them play and sing.

17. And Jesus taught the common people of Lahore; he healed their sick, and showed to them the way to rise to better things by helpfulness.

18. He said, We are not rich by what we get and hold; the only things we keep are those we give away.

19. If you would live the perfect life, give forth your life in service for your kind, and for the forms of life that men esteem the lower forms of life.

20. But Jesus could not tarry longer in Lahore; he bade the priests and other friends farewell; and then he took his camel and he went his way toward the Sind.

The Aquarian Gospel, ch.37[9b]

Jesus in India once more! This time he is told of in a typical "biblical style" with a traditional division of the text into chapters and verses. More than in Notovitch's *Life of Saint Issa*, Jesus here is given the features of an Indian guru, as when he teaches the Brahmin Ajainin about reincarnation. This time he does not limit his travels to the East but also visits Greece and Egypt.

Not only is the theological content very different from that of the New Testament: a reading soon reveals that this cannot be an authentic writing from early Christian times. The fact that Jesus visits Leh, the capital of Ladakh, reminds us that it was in the monastery of Hemis near this city that Notovitch made his alleged discovery. The fact that Jesus continues to Lahore, however, does not make the impression more favorable, for this city was not known in history until the seventh century A.D.

The Aquarian Gospel contains a great number of historical mistakes, which show that the author had no primary knowledge of the matters he wrote about. In the very first verse of this Gospel (1:1), he confused King Herod the Great with Herod Antipas. Other personages appear with strange names which seem to have arisen by misreadings. The Egyptian priest Matheno (13:4 etc.) reminds us of his colleague Manetho in the third century B.C. In chapter 36, Jesus encounters the wise Chinese Meng-ste, who is probably

76

meant to be Meng-tse.[99] This Chinese philosopher, commonly called Mencius, also belongs to another time than that of Jesus (about 300 B.C.). In chapter 38, Jesus visits "the three wise men." That the Magi numbered just three is not related in the Gospel of Matthew but is a later tradition. One of them is named Kaspar, a name not known in this context until the Middle Ages.

No, *The Aquarian Gospel* is no genuine biblical writing and even has no real pretentions to be. There is no story here about a manuscript hidden in Tibet or elsewhere, and the author admits quite openly that he got the writing from direct inspiration. Thus, this is a more honest book than many others of the same kind.

The author, or transmittor, was Levi H. Dowling (1844–1911), who preferred to call himself just Levi.[100] His father was a preacher of the Disciples of Christ, and Levi also began a career as a preacher at the age of sixteen. At eighteen he was pastor of a small congregation, and he served as a chaplain during the Civil War. He was active in publishing Sunday school literature but later turned to the medical profession. He is said to have graduated from two colleges and to have practiced medicine for a number of years. He claimed to have prepared himself for forty years with prayer and meditation, until he was ready to receive the message, and when the revelations began to flow, he retired from medicine and spent his time writing down what he had received. *The Aquarian Gospel* was the crown of his life; it was published in 1911, the year of his death.

Levi believed himself to have established contact with the Akashic Records, a cosmic memory often mentioned in theosophical literature. Through this communication he received higher knowledge of the biblical events and could transmit his knowledge in a new Gospel. He received his Gospel in the early morning hours, between two and six, and seems to have written down his messages immediately, in the same way that Joseph Smith did. The procedure has been poetically described in a work of his entitled *The Cusp of the Ages*, parts of which have been published in the foreword to the modern American editions. Here we learn that Levi was commissioned by Visel, the Goddess of Wisdom, who sent him into her "record galleries" to read and write.

Like Joseph Smith, Levi was conscious of his special role as a prophet to a new age. Just as Jacob prophesies the coming of Joseph Smith in the latter's version of Genesis, so the wise Elihu foretells the coming of Levi in the future:

> And when the world is ready to receive, lo, God will send a messenger to open up the book and copy from its sacred pages all the messages of Purity and Love [7:26].

For Levi this was a message foretelling a new era in the history of mankind, the Aquarian age. He introduced a theme that was to become popular much later in the new religious movements of the 1960s. It was at that time that the idea received a new hearing at the entrance of a new era, "The Age of Aquarius." By the so-called precession the position of the spring equinox moves backwards through the zodiac. At the time of Jesus it passed from the sign of Aries to that of Pisces, and in our time, almost 2,000 years later, it has entered the sign of Aquarius. To many astrologers, this means that a new era with a new religion is at hand.

Even if *The Aquarian Gospel* does not claim to be a document from early Christianity, it has the appearance of a biblical writing, with 22 sections, 182 chapters, and division into verses. It has also been used as a holy scripture by various religious groups. It is said to be widely read in the Spiritualist Church of the U.S.A., and even to have found its way into the services of the Ancient Catholic Church, an English religious body that enjoyed short-lived fame in Chelsea after World War II.[101] Together with *The Book of Mormon* and *The Gospel of Peace*, it is probably the most widespread of the neobiblical writings of our time.

Extracts from the Gospel have sometimes been presented as genuine Christian traditions by authors less concerned with historical truth. As we have seen, it was quoted by Nicholas Roerich as an example of living popular traditions in Ladakh. Mystifications of this kind show that Dowling's work is not quite as innocuous as it might seem.

As we have already seen, Levi was not entirely unaffected by earlier attempts of the same kind. He certainly had read or heard of Notovitch. The description of the sevenfold initiation of Jesus in Heliopolis (chapters 47–55) has slight but unmistakable resemblance to the description of an initiation into the mysteries of Isis, given by Apuleius in his novel *The Golden Ass:*

1. The work of Jesus in the Chamber of the Dead was done, and in the temple purple room he stood before the hierophant.
2. And he was clothed in purple robes; and all the brothers stood. The hierophant arose and said,
3. This is a royal day for all the hosts of Israel. In honor of their chosen son we celebrate the great Passover Feast.
4. And then he said to Jesus, Brother, man, most excellent of men, in all the temple tests you have won out.
5. Six times before the bar of right you have been judged; six times you have received the highest honors man can give; and now you stand prepared to take the last degree.
6. Upon your brow I place this diadem, and in the Great Lodge of the heavens and earth you are THE CHRIST.
7. This is your great Passover rite. You are a neophyte no more; but now a master mind.
8. Now, man can do no more; but God himself will speak, and will confirm your title and degree.
9. Go on your way, for you must preach the gospel of good will to men and peace on earth; must open up the prison doors and set the captives free.
10. And while the hierophant yet spoke the temple bells rang out; a pure white dove descended from above and sat on Jesus' head.
11. And then a voice that shook the very temple said, THIS IS THE CHRIST; and every living creature said, AMEN.
12. The great doors of the temple swung ajar; the Logos journeyed on his way to a conqueror. [Chapter 55][102]

Here as so often in *The Aquarian Gospel*, Jesus is given features strangely well known from other literature. Still more than in *The Life of Saint Issa*, Jesus becomes a wisdom-seeking traveler, who journeys from place to place in order to establish contact with other teachers and to be initiated in their deep secrets. It is a kind of personality that Eliza Butler has called "the Magus."[103] This kind of person is well known from the literature of antiquity. In just the same way the neopythagorean Apollonius of Tyana (first century A.D.) set off to India and learned the wisdom of the Brahmins, visited the naked philosophers of Egypt, and during a stay in Greece was initiated into the Eleusinian mysteries.

79

The idea of having Jesus initiated into an Oriental mystery cult is probably not taken directly from the literature of antiquity. The motif of the traveling seeker of wisdom and of proper initiations also recurs in the Renaissance. Christian Rosencreutz, the alleged founder of the Rosicrucian Society, is said to have journeyed in the Orient to gather its wisdom before he organized his brotherhood.[104] In the eighteenth century similar things were told about the mysterious Count of Saint-Germain, who was said to have traveled in the Orient and to have been initiated into various mysteries.[105] The romantic story of the secret Egyptian order is well known from Mozart's, or rather Emanuel Schikaneder's, *The Magic Flute*, inspired by Masonic rites. There is a similar story in the *The Essene Letter*, although the travel motif is less prominent there. Obviously Dowling belonged to circles where secret initiations were highly appreciated.

In one respect *The Aquarian Gospel* differs considerably from *The Essene Letter* and from many other modern apocrypha. Dowling believed in the bodily resurrection of Christ, and he has Jesus appear not only to his disciples but also — "fully materialized" — to the Indian priest Ravanna in Orissa and to the magian priests in Persepolis. The latter city was destroyed forever during the stay of Alexander the Great in 330 B.C., but in this context there is no place for pettiness. In this Gospel, Jesus also rescues the Roman Claudas and his wife from a storm on the Tiber!

The Aquarian Gospel may best be understood as a work of fiction, an attempt to use the author's fantasy to add new features to the image of Jesus, features taken from a tradition that Dowling felt connected with. Since the result is poor, his claims of a heavenly inspiration seem a little presumptuous. Whichever were the cosmic forces that Dowling communicated with, they were unable to produce more than a fairly faint bible pastiche, even if it contains some fantastic features.

12

The Diligent Dr. Szekely

And then many sick and maimed came to Jesus, asking him: "If you know all things, tell us, why do we suffer with these grievous plagues? Why are we not whole like other men? Master, heal us, that we too may be made strong, and need abide no longer in our misery. We know that you have it in your power to heal all manner of disease. Free us from Satan and from all his great afflictions. Master, have compassion on us."

And Jesus answered: "Happy are you, that you hunger for the truth, for I will satisfy you with the bread of wisdom. Happy are you, that you knock, for I will open to you the door of life. Happy are you, that you would cast off the power of Satan, for I will lead you into the kingdom of our Mother's angels, where the power of Satan cannot enter."

And they asked him in amazement: "Who is our Mother and which her angels? And where is her kingdom?"

"Your mother is in you, and you in her. She bore you; she gives you life. It was she who gave to you your body, and to her shall you one day give it back again. Happy are you when you come to know her and her kingdom; if you receive your Mother's angels and if you do her laws. I tell you truly, he who does these things shall never see disease. For the power of our Mother is above all. And it destroys Satan and his kingdom, and has rule over all your bodies and all living things.

"The blood which runs in us is born of the blood of our Earthly Mother. Her blood falls from the clouds; leaps up from the womb of the earth; babbles in the brooks of the mountains; flows wide in the rivers of the plains; sleeps in the lakes; rages mightily in the tempestuous seas.

"The air which we breathe is born of the breath of our Earthly Mother. Her breath is azure in the heights of the heavens; soughs in the tops of the mountains; whispers in the leaves of the forest; billows over the cornfields; slumbers in the deep valleys; burns hot in the desert.

"The hardness of our bones is born of the bones of our Earthly Mother, of the rocks and of the stones. They stand naked to the heavens on the tops of mountains; are as giants that lie sleeping on

81

the sides of the mountains, as idols set in the desert, and are hidden in the deepness of the earth.

"The tenderness of our flesh is born of the flesh of our Earthly Mother, whose flesh waxes yellow and red in the fruits of the trees, and nurtures us in the furrows of the fields.

"Our bowels are born of the bowels of our Earthly Mother, and are hid from our eyes, like the invisible depths of the earth.

"The light of our eyes, the hearing of our ears, both are born of the colors and the sounds of the Earthly Mother; which enclose us about, as the waves of the sea a fish, as the eddying air a bird.

"I tell you in very truth, Man is the Son of the Earthly Mother, and from her did the Son of Man receive his whole body, even as the body of the newborn babe is born of the womb of his mother. I tell you truly, you are one with the Earthly Mother; she is in you, and you in her. Of her were you born, in her do you live, and to her you shall return again. Keep, therefore, her laws, for none can live long, neither be happy, but he who honors his Earthly Mother and does her laws. For your breath is her breath; your blood her blood; your bone her bone; your flesh her flesh; your bowels her bowels; your eyes and your ears are her eyes and her ears.

The beginning of The Gospel of Peace

Some may find this text rather attractive. It has a certain artistic quality and a freshness usually lacking in this kind of literature. The romantic feeling for the beauty of nature is restricted by the literary form with its recurring reiterations, more resembling Indian than biblical poetry.

Except for *The Book of Mormon, The Gospel of Peace* is perhaps the most widespread writing that we shall discuss, for if we may believe the advertisements of the publisher, more than 400,000 copies have been sold.[106] Probably its most enthusiastic readers are young Americans with an interest in environment and health food and with a susceptibility to new and unconventional religious ideas.

We have astonishingly exact information about the alleged manuscripts of this book. Two complete manuscripts are said to exist: one in Old Slavonic belonging to the National Library of Vienna; the second in Aramaic belonging to the Archivio Segreto, the secret archives of the Vatican, which contain large collections of manuscripts. Furthermore, some Hebrew fragments are said to have existed in the Benedictine Monastery of Monte Cassino in Middle Italy.

Anyone who tries to find these manuscripts in ordinary catalogues, however, is likely to do his research in vain. All information about the manuscripts comes from only one person, a health food-minded doctor of Hungarian and French extraction. His name was Edmond Bordeaux Szekely, and he spent the last part of his life in San Diego, California, where he was the leader of a "biogenic" institute. His practice was obviously prosperous, for the catalogue of the institute is lavishly produced, and the new editions of *The Gospel of Peace* abound in illustrations (mainly well-known woodcuts or prints by Gustave Doré). Besides the various editions of *The Gospel of Peace*, Szekely has also published about sixty books mainly about health food.

The publication of *The Gospel of Peace* has a long and complicated history, and every attempt to describe it is obstructed by terminological confusion. When the book was first published, in England in 1937, it bore the title *The Gospel of Peace by the disciple John*. Szekely's English publisher, C. W. Daniel, has continued to print the book with this title until now. Szekely said in the preface of the 1937 edition that it was only part of the content of the manuscripts, but that the publication should continue. Nothing more was published, however, until 1974 (!) when two more volumes appeared. These two later volumes are entitled *The Gospel of the Essenes* in the English edition, but in the American edition all three volumes are called *The Essene Gospel of Peace*. The question is whether *The Gospel of Peace* should refer to the first volume only or to all three volumes, as in the American edition. I choose the latter alternative, because all the material should, according to Szekely, come from the same manuscripts.

Who then was this Dr. Szekely, who claimed to be a palaeographer, a philologist and a health food specialist in the same person, and who showed such impressive diligence at his desk during his long career?[107] In a fairly recent book, *The Discovery of The Essene Gospel of Peace* (1977), which is said to clear up all the problems about the finds, there is also some personal information about Szekely. He was the son of a Transylvanian of Unitarian beliefs and his French Catholic wife. He stated that his grandfather was the Hungarian poet Alexander Székely, Unitarian bishop of Cluj, and among his forefathers he also reckoned the well-known

traveler and philologist Alexander Csoma de Körös.[108] Szekely was
sent to a Catholic school, run by the Piarist order; with the help
of the headmaster, Monsignor Mondik, he continued his studies in
Rome with Monsignor Angelo Mercati, who was at that time the
Prefect of the Secret Archives.[109] It was here that he claims to have
discovered the Aramaic manuscript at some time between 1923 and
1924; during a visit to Monte Cassino he also claims to have found
Hebrew fragments corresponding with the Aramaic text.[110]

More precise details about these finds are lacking, and the events
are totally wrapped in mist by Szekely's romantic narrative, which
gives many impressions of nature and the environment but hardly
any information about what he in fact was doing. The central event,
the find of the Aramaic manuscript, is almost forgotten, and it is
only mentioned incidentally when Szekely tells the story of the
Monte Cassino fragments. There is thus no description of the
manuscript, and we are not told whether it might have been a scroll
or a codex (an ordinary book, sewn in the back). The former
possibility is perhaps the most likely one, but is by no means certain.

Reading through such a large Aramaic manuscript is a difficult
task demanding months of work. The copying is in itself an extensive procedure with many difficulties. Szekely, however, never
seems to have had any problems with this. He just "read" the
manuscript in 1923 in Monsignor Mercati's study, which obviously
was sufficient, for shortly afterwards, he tells us, he said goodbye
to Mercati and never saw him any more. How could he then obtain access to the text? Did he carry photocopies with him in his
baggage when he left (something he forgets to mention)? Not even
today, with our sophisticated phototechnology, would it be possible to produce copies useful for a scholarly edition in such haste.
Perhaps the University of Paris could have provided some information, for Szekely claims to have presented his finds there in 1925,
but his dissertation is said to have been lost, and the name of the
professor who assessed his research is not known.[111]

Nor is there any hope for a scholarly edition of the Hebrew,
Aramaic, and Old Slavonic texts. Szekely says that he had devoted
a great deal of work to this edition, but that he put it all aside when
his "friend" Aldous Huxley told him that it all seemed dull and

unreadable. Scholarly editors of texts should perhaps take care not to seek the advice of novelists.[112]

The greatest lack of information concerns the Old Slavonic manuscript.[113] When did Szekely go to Vienna to study it? His German translator, Werner Zimmerman, who has also translated *The Gospel of the Holy Twelve* into German, and who is not quite reliable as an informant, states that Szekely found the Old Slavonic version first and later the Aramaic one. This does not agree with Szekely's own account, for he tells us that he went to Paris and Leipzig to buy Aramaic and Hebrew dictionaries on his way to Rome, and does not mention a stop in Vienna on his route. In fact, the Vienna manuscript is not mentioned at all in the book that is intended to answer all questions about *The Gospel of Peace!*

The Old Slavonic text is said to be a translation from the Aramaic one, and perhaps Szekely has discarded it as irrelevant. Why, however, is it mentioned on the title page of the first part of *The Gospel of Peace* together with the Aramaic text? The catalogue of Szekely's books enumerates the many languages that he claimed to know but does not say a word about any knowledge of Slavic languages.

The title page of the two later volumes of *The Gospel of Peace* does not mention the Old Slavonic texts, but states instead that the translation was made from original Hebrew and Aramaic texts. The Hebrew fragments from Monte Cassino thus seem to have been introduced here, although they are never mentioned in the editions themselves. The only information about them comes from Szekely's book about the discovery. What he tells there is as nebulous as the story of the Aramaic text; there is no information about how many alleged fragments there were.

Szekely has indeed published a Hebrew text, supposedly that of the Monte Cassino fragments, although he never indicates the provenance of his text. I do not know of any American edition of this work, but in the English edition of the two latter parts called *The Gospel of the Essenes*, there are fifteen pages with a nonvocalized Hebrew text, which prove to be the entire first part of *The Gospel of Peace*, although with some omissions and differences. There is no translation, nor any commentary, and nothing indicates that this is a reconstruction from fragments. Szekely tells us that he found the fragments in 1924, and that at that time he considered them to be the source of the Aramaic text. If he possessed this fairly complete text, however, why did he not use it for his first edition in 1937, and why did he not even mention it? How could he be content with the Aramaic translation and with the still later Old Slavonic one?

I have been helped with my study of Szekely's Hebrew text by a competent Hebrew scholar, who has said that the language of the text is correct Hebrew of a postbiblical period, similar to that found in the Mishnah.[114] That sounds impressive. But having a Hebrew text is really not the same as possessing a Hebrew original. As we have seen, Szekely has never published a word of either the Aramaic or the Old Slavonic version. The credibility of his more recent presentation of a Hebrew version, hereto unknown, may be left to the judgment of the reader.

Let us imagine that Szekely never had any original text at all but wrote it all himself in English (or in French or in Hungarian, that makes no difference). Moreover, people around him are not satisfied with the "translation" but insist on seeing the original texts. What then is to be done? In order to show his alleged originals he has to find translators who can translate the work *into* these languages, and that is a risky task. If there exist any persons at all in our time who are able and willing to make translations into Bible Aramaic or Old Slavonic, they must be extremely rare indeed. On the other hand, it is not difficult to find a learned speaker of Hebrew who can make a translation into acceptable Hebrew, for the difference between biblical Hebrew and the spoken language of today is not so great. Let us imagine that Szekely knew such a person willing to make the translation. In that way he has obtained an "original text," which he may claim to have had in his possession since the 1920s, though he has forgotten to tell about it!

It is perhaps relevant that the Hebrew fragments were found in Monte Cassino. Szekely cannot have been unaware of the fact that the monastery was bombed and destroyed during World War II, and that a possible Gospel manuscript would not have stood a great chance of survival. Thus, he would have been able to cover up his tracks.

More oddities exist. When *The Gospel of Peace* was published for the first time in 1937, Szekely said in his preface that he had only had time to translate an eighth of the text, but that he was pursuing his work. The same promise was repeated in later editions; further, when Werner Zimmermann paid a visit to Szekely in Tecate in 1949, he was promised a copy of the entire manuscript, but this promise was never fulfilled.[115] As we have already seen, it was not until the 1970s that a continuation was published. At the same time the first part (that printed in 1937) came out in an American edition. It has a preface which is dated 1937 but is in fact considerably altered. In this edition this first part of the work is no longer said to be an eighth of the manuscript but a *third*, which implies that the three volumes are meant to contain the entire text of the manuscripts. Perhaps it has been beyond Szekely's undeniable powers to produce five more volumes.

That an eighth has become a third is not the only change slipped into the preface of the American edition. In the original preface from 1937, the Aramaic manuscript is dated to the first century, and this statement stands in an English reprint from 1977, in which the preface is left without any change. But in the 1974 American edition, the manuscript is dated to the *third* century, naturally without any indication that Szekely had some reason to change his mind about its age.

Still more conspicuous is that some polemical passages in the original preface have been omitted in the American one.[116] Originally, it was stated that the words of Jesus had been half-forgotten, that they were not collected until some generations after they were uttered, that they had been misunderstood, wrongly annotated, and so on. The two editors, Szekely and Lawrence Purcell Weaver, declared it their heavy responsibility "to proclaim the present New Testament . . . as deformed and falsified." All this has disappeared from the preface of the American edition, although it is still dated 1937.

The first edition from 1937 had the title *The Gospel of Peace of the disciple John,* and the same title has been used in the many English reprints.[117] In the American edition, however, John has disappeared as the author of the first part. On the other hand, the Essenes have made their entry in the English as well as the American

87

edition of volumes two and three. The Dead Sea Scrolls were discovered in 1947, and the two later volumes of Szekely's publications contain various "fragments," with content resembling those writings. Volume 2 contains parts of the Dead Sea Scrolls, said to have parallels in the "Gospel" and also mentions the Teacher of Righteousness, a well-known figure from the scrolls. The content of the manuscripts thus appears not to be Gospel — except the first part, published in 1937 — and the remaining part is a collection of fragments.

This is again very odd, for until the 1970s Szekely never spoke about any fragments (except the Hebrew Monte Cassino fragments, which are obviously meant to contain the *first* part of the text). How is it possible that the two latter parts of the Gospel have been transformed into a collection of fragments? Perhaps this part of the manuscript contains copies of earlier fragments? The manuscripts would in that case begin with *The Gospel of Peace* and then continue with copies of old fragments. It just happens that Szekely did not observe this, although he translated the text to exactly the point where the "Gospel" ended and the "fragments" began. What a pity that he did not go on reading one or two sentences more!

Let us further note that the coeditor from 1937, Lawrence Purcell Weaver, had been ungratefully left out of the American edition. He was mainly known as an author of books about health food and cosmotherapy and seems to have been of little use for a translation from Old Slavonic and Aramaic.[118]

Manuscripts preserved in Vienna and in Rome should be fairly easy to obtain. So far, however, nobody has seen them except Szekely, and he gives not the slightest indication that would help someone else find them.[119] Manuscripts in official libraries always have code numbers; if Szekely has been working with the manuscripts for half a century, it should be his moral duty to inform others where they are catalogued. But this is not the case. Although these manuscripts would be of tremendous value — comparable with the Dead Sea Scrolls or the Nag-Hammadi library — it is impossible to acquire the slightest bit of evidence for their existence even from the libraries themselves.

I have been informed by the National Library of Vienna that inquiries about the Old Slavonic manuscript are not uncommon, but that it is completely unknown there, and the general opinion is that it was made up by Szekely. Nor is the manuscript listed in Gerhard Birkfellner's extensive catalogue of Old Slavonic manuscripts in Austria.[120]

I have received an equally negative answer from Rome in a letter from Monsignor Martino Giusti, the present Prefect of the Secret Archives, where Szekely claimed to have made his great discovery. Monsignor Giusti states categorically that there is no such Aramaic Gospel manuscript in the Archives, and that Szekely's name is missing from the card index, where all visitors to the Archives are registered.[121] That implies that Szekely never did any research there, and thus cannot have made his alleged discovery either. From this fact and from the many untruths and contradictions we have encountered, we may draw the certain conclusion that *The Gospel of Peace* is a sheer forgery, written entirely by Szekely himself. It is one of the strangest frauds we know of in the biblical field, as it has been carried through by stages during a whole lifetime and has been built into an entire body of research, based on imagination only. The discovery of the Dead Sea Scrolls gave Szekely fresh ideas for his later publications, which shows that his forgery has been going on for a considerable time.

His work is not entirely without interest, however. As we have seen, Szekely's "Gospel" is not entirely devoid of literary merit though the book proves fairly monotonous during a lengthy reading, just as its high-pitched tone tends to be enervating. The constant idea, also appearing in the later "fragments," is that Jesus taught not only about the heavenly Father but also about an earthly Mother, a Mother Earth, who is the origin and goal of nature. Man is a child of the Father and the Mother:

> It is by love that the Heavenly Father and the Earthly Mother and the Son of Man become one. For the spirit of the Son of Man was created from the spirit of the Heavenly Father, and his body from the body of the Earthly Mother. Become, therefore, perfect as the spirit of your Heavenly Father and the body of your Earthly Mother are perfect. And so love your Heavenly Father, as he loves your spirit. And so love your Earthly Mother, as she loves your body. And so love your true brothers, as your Heavenly Father and your Earthly Mother love them.[122]

89

As you may remember, *The Gospel of the Holy Twelve* proclaims God as a Father-Mother; there are many today who may appreciate this concept, and think that God cannot be spoken of in masculine terms only. Szekely's work proposes something different. Here Jesus speaks about *two* divinities, a male and a female one, and this seems unacceptable to the general Bible reader. Jesus stands entirely in the Jewish tradition with its commandment, "You shall not have any gods but me." If Jesus had preached the belief in two divinities, he would quite certainly have been judged a preacher of false gods, but no such accusations against him are known.

Except for the parts taken from the Dead Sea Scrolls, *The Gospel of Peace* does not appear to come from the Palestinian milieu, but reveals itself as a modern composition interspersed with expressions from the Sermon on the Mount such as "Happy are you," "become perfect," and "our Heavenly Father." The impression that it lacks authenticity is strengthened by the romantic metaphors of nature: the water *sleeps* in the lakes, the air *whispers* in the leaves of the forest, etc. A reader interested in matters of style may compare it with the nature Psalms 104 and 147, which show what real biblical nature poetry is like.

Szekely's main interest is not to introduce a poetic element in the teachings of Jesus, however. As in *The Gospel of the Holy Twelve*, it is the bodily health of man that is in the center. The heavenly Father takes care of those things that are spiritual, but the earthly Mother and the body are of equal importance. With the help of air, water, and sunshine, the body of man has to be cleansed of all evil-smelling filth and to be reborn to a fuller life. In this context, we find a somewhat astonishing instruction for an enema, which is elevated to religious significance:

> Seek, therefore, a large trailing gourd, having a stalk the length of a man; take out its inwards and fill it with water from the river which the sun has warmed. Hang it upon the branch of a tree, and kneel upon the ground before the angel of water, and suffer the end of the stalk of the trailing gourd to enter your hinder parts, that the water may flow through all your bowels. Afterwards rest kneeling on the ground before the angel of water and pray to the living God that he will forgive you all your past sins, and pray the angel of water that he will free your body, that it may carry away from within it all the unclean and evil-smelling things of Satan. And you shall see

with your eyes and smell with your nose all the abominations and uncleannesses which defiled the temple of your body; even all the sins which abode in your body, tormenting you with all manner of pains. I tell you truly, baptism with water frees you from all these.[123]

Szekely's main interest obviously belonged to the physical rather than the spiritual level. Like *The Gospel of the Holy Twelve*, his work may be seen as commendable health propaganda, here vested in a poetic form with a biblical connection. Why should it be impossible to write a book of that kind and to preach about environmental questions, about sound living, and about man's affinity with nature in a tone of solemn revelation? What is dubious about Szekely is that he — not unlike Joseph Smith — refused to admit that his revelation came entirely from himself but had to mask it behind alleged finds of manuscripts.

It is a psychological enigma that Szekely, with his indisputable writing skill, was unable to propagandize such self-evident matters as clean water, clean air, and sunshine without yielding to frauds and mystifications. Certain features of his character indicate an insatiable urge for self-assertion. He was eager to claim relationship with prominent literary ancestors and friendship with the famous, such as Mercati, Huxley, and also Romain Rolland, whom he regarded as a cofounder of his biogenic society. That he really knew any of these remains to be proven. His alleged but entirely undocumented knowledge of Old Slavonic, Sanskrit, Aramaic, and Hebrew is evidently intended to give his words weight and authority. He also showed a surprising interest in the circulation figures of his books, which scholarly and religious writers otherwise used to speak more modestly about. His psychological type is not unlike that of some other religious leaders with high personal pretensions. Joseph Smith and Mirza Ghulam Ahmad are just two examples.

13

*The Stolen Scroll
from Masada*

The borderline between fraud and fiction has often been vague in Jesus literature, and sometimes the reader is at a loss to decide the difference. Donovan Joyce's *The Jesus Scroll* is a good example.[124] It is an unpleasant book, and I have hesitated to include it in my collection of modern apocrypha. But the book exists, and some readers may think that it is a realistic account of true events. Let us, then, take the book and its author as they are.

The background of the story is the famous excavations of Masada, the last stronghold of the Jewish Zealots; it survived the fall of Jerusalem in A.D. 70 and was captured by the Romans in the spring of A.D. 73 after two years of siege. Thorough excavations took place from 1963 to 1965 under the leadership of the well-known archaeologist Yigael Yadin.[125] Fragments of fourteen scrolls were found there; this is now considered the most important discovery of Jewish texts after the Dead Sea Scrolls. Thus we have fragments from the Old Testament, from apocrypha, and from writings similar to the Qumran texts. And now for the story.

Joyce says that he went to Israel in December 1964 in order to gather material for a book. For this purpose, he also tried to get access to the site at Masada but was denied permission to visit the site. As he relates it, he was haughtily treated by Yadin and his wife, and to make matters worse, he was persecuted by unknown agents, who pestered him by plugging up his toilet in the hotel!

Joyce's futile efforts to get into Masada were eventually rewarded, however, and quite unexpectedly, at the Tel Aviv airport. There he experienced a dramatic encounter with a new acquaintance, a "Professor Max Grosset," who, according to Joyce himself, appeared to be using a false name. This gentleman now revealed to Joyce that he had managed to get into the site at Masada, and that he had also managed to steal a well-preserved scroll, which he had found in an earthenware jar on the site. He now offered Joyce $5,000 to smuggle the scroll out of Israel.

The reported dialogue in the airport gives an impression of the general style of Joyce's book:

> "You're right, you know, Joyce . . . and you're all sorts of a clever bastard for foxing it out . . . but something *has* been found down there, although you're wrong in thinking that the Yadins know exactly what it is."
>
> "How could they bloody help knowing?"
>
> "Because I didn't bloody tell them," was his cool reply. "You see, I was the finder! It was at the end of last season, in fact, the very last day of it. I was working alone and . . . well, let's just say that I found something I didn't report."
>
> "Like what?" He looked hard at me for a couple of seconds before he said: "It was an earthen-ware jar . . . very old and possibly valuable. I decided to stick to it!"
>
> "You were going to steal an empty jar?"
>
> Grosset gave a derisive snort. "Steal it, my crutch," he said, somewhat inelegantly. "Stealing is taking something belonging to someone else. The jar didn't belong to anyone; it had lain in the earth of Masada for damned near two thousand years, and no matter what the Yadins might say — or the bloody Department of Antiquities — it belonged to absolutely nobody until I found it . . . and then it belonged to me!"

That it was not an empty jar was of course revealed to Joyce immediately.

No business deal took place, however, and Grosset disappeared for an unknown destination in a taxi with the scroll in his baggage. Before they parted, Joyce had the chance to look at the stolen treasure. Grosset took him to the men's lavatories in the airport and unrolled the parchment manuscript, which was ten or twelve feet long. He also told Joyce about its sensational contents, for obviously he had already had time to decipher and translate the Aramaic text. The scroll turned out to have been written in the night before the fall of Masada on 15 April A.D. 73, and the author said he was Jesus of Gennesareth. He was eighty years old, the son of a certain Jacob and the last of the Maccabaean dynasty. He had seen his own son crucified by the Romans and now understood that his own death was at hand at the capture of the stronghold.

Yadin himself denied Grosset's story in a letter, which is also printed in the book. He refers to the condition of the fragments found in Masada, for there were no entire scrolls found, as in Qumran, but only loose fragments. Also, the description of the scroll seems more than permissibly suspect. Anyone who knows anything about antique scrolls will immediately understand that such a scroll could not have been unrolled to the length of ten to twelve feet in this careless way without breaking. The scroll, if it ever existed except in the mind of the author, cannot therefore be genuine. In addition, the man who showed it pretended to be a thief and appeared under a false name, and his statements about the content — communicated in a men's lavatory — certainly cannot be accepted without reservation.

Of course, Joyce cannot guarantee that Grosset's interpretation of the text is correct; instead, throughout he bases his reasoning on a hypothetical perhaps, "imagine if it is true!" He does not doubt that this is "a time bomb for Christianity." It is self-evident to Joyce that Jesus (or rather Jehoshua or Jeshu) of Gennesareth is identical to Jesus of Nazareth. He cites evidence that Jesus was a descendant of the Maccabees, that he was never crucified, and that he lived to the age of eighty, when he was killed together with many others in Masada.

Even *if* the scroll should really exist, and *if* it should be genuine, and *if* Grosset's translation should be correct, there would nevertheless be no reason to identify the author of the writing as Jesus. Jehoshua/Jeshu was a common name; that his father's name was Jacob, and that he lived himself to the age of eighty indicate that he must have been a different person.

The same may be said about the designation "Jesus of Gennesareth." Gennesareth lay on the narrow coastal strip to the west of the Sea of Galilee (see Mark 6:53). Jesus never appears in Jewish or Christian literature under that designation, and his home town, Nazareth, was farther to the west.

Perhaps the whole thing is just a novel about a great journalistic scoop, yet there are many circumstances contradicting this interpretation. The publisher included it in a series of nonfiction, and the author constantly introduces real persons — Professor and Mrs.

Yadin and others—in a way suggesting that the book is a report of real events.

Joyce certainly looks for signs that this "time bomb" is soon to explode. He asks why a Soviet Russian Ilyushin aircraft was standing ready for take-off at Tel Aviv, when Grosset disappeared. And what did President Podgorny have in mind when he paid a visit to Pope Paul VI in 1967? Did he perhaps tell the pope that he was now the possessor of the scroll? Why did the Vatican show sympathy to the Arabs rather than to Israel in the Middle East conflict? Was it in exchange for a promise from the Russians to keep silent about the scroll? So the speculations go on, never with any foothold in reality but always presented in a tone suggesting that great events are at hand.

The aim of the whole thing may remain obscure. Perhaps the book was written only in revenge against Yadin and his wife for not letting Joyce into the site at Masada? Perhaps he found consolation in the thought that somebody pulled Yadin's leg and deprived him of a most fantastic treasure that could have changed the history of Christianity as well as the developing conflict in the Middle East. In that case, it is an entirely new variant of the marvelous book discovery so attractive to fiction writers of all times.

14

Was Jesus a Magician?

We now arrive at a writing more difficult to assess than any others discussed in this book. It is by no means certain that *The Secret Gospel of Mark* is a modern forgery; many scholars still seem to take it for granted that it comes from early Christian times. Its discovery is so wrapped in mystery and has been presented in such a sensational way, however, that it cannot be left out.[127]

Over the years, it has been suggested from time to time in the world press, that there exists a Gospel fragment showing that Jesus was a homosexual. Moreover, this suggestion did not originate with just anybody, but comes from an internationally famous scholar, Professor Morton Smith of Columbia University, New York. He himself has presented his discovery and his theories about it in two books, one scholarly, the other more popular and sensational; it is on these two books that the entire discussion is based.

Morton Smith made his find as early as 1958, in the monastery of Mar Saba, some twelve miles southeast of Jerusalem. This monastery is situated in the wilderness of Judea, and its library, which is stored in a tower, is generally inaccessible to occasional visitors. Smith, however, was granted permission by the patriarch to spend two weeks in the monastery in order to study the manuscripts he found and to catalogue them. He then published a catalogue of the manuscripts in the periodical of the Jerusalem Patriarchate in 1960, and also did scholarly editions of some of the manuscripts that he came across.

Among the books that Smith found in the library was a copy of the *Letters of St. Ignatius*, in Isaac Voss's printed edition from 1646. The manuscript in question was found on the two last blank pages and on the inside back cover. Here somebody had written down in a mideighteenth-century hand what seemed to be a letter from Clement of Alexandria (circa A.D. 200). Smith photographed the three pages, and they are now printed in facsimile in one of his books.[128] Since Smith left the monastery library, nothing more seems to have been seen of the manuscript. It has now been out of sight for more than twenty years.

Analysis of the language of the text suggests that it contains a letter by Clement hitherto completely unknown. Its choice of words and its linguistic structure agree with Clement's usage. When an edition of the manuscript was published in 1973, it seemed that a letter by Clement had indeed been discovered, although some scholars disagreed.[129]

This brief letter, the ending of which appears to be lost, is of special interest because it contains an extract from an unknown Gospel said to have been written by Mark. Unlike the canonical Gospel of Mark, this is said to be a secret Gospel, preserved in the Christian community, but only accessible to "those who are being initiated into the great mysteries," whatever that might be. It is also said that this Gospel had been appropriated by a Gnostic sect, the Carpocratians, who falsified it by adding some insertions. In his letter, Clement thus wants to inform his addressee, Theodorus, about the content of the original text and about the Gnostic falsifications. The excerpt from the Gospel is so brief that it can be rendered in its entirety:

> To you, therefore, I shall not hesitate to answer the questions you have asked, refuting the falsifications by the very words of the Gospel. For example, after "And they were in the road going up to Jerusalem," and what follows, until "After three days he shall arise," the secret Gospel brings the following material word for word: "And they come into Bethany. And a certain woman whose brother had died was there. And, coming, she prostrated herself before Jesus and says to him, 'Son of David, have mercy on me.' But the disciples rebuked her. And Jesus, being angered, went off with her into the garden where the tomb was, and straightway a great cry was heard from the tomb. And going near Jesus rolled away the stone from the door of the tomb. And straightway, going in where the youth was, he stretched forth his hand and raised him, seizing his hand. But the youth, looking upon him, loved him and began to beseech him that he might be with him. And going out of the tomb they came into the house of the youth, for he was rich. And after six days Jesus told him what to do and [in] the evening the youth comes to

him, wearing a linen cloth over his naked body. And he remained with him that night, for Jesus taught him the mystery of the kingdom of God. And thence, arising, he returned to the other side of the Jordan."

After these words follows the text, "And James and John come to him," and all that section. But "naked man with naked man," and the other things about which you wrote, are not found.

And after the words, "And he comes into Jericho," the secret Gospel adds only, "And the sister of the youth whom Jesus loved and his mother and Salome were there, and Jesus did not receive them." But the many other things about which you wrote both seem to be and are falsifications.

This brief Gospel fragment does not seem very sensational. It mostly reminds us of the story of the raising of Lazarus in John 11:1–44, although the details are different.[130] We do not see much of the alleged homosexuality; there is no indication that the relationship between Jesus and the youth would be of that kind, and the compromising words "naked man with naked man" are said by Clement himself in the text *not* to belong to the original Gospel but to be an insertion by the Carpocratians. A certain deal of imagination on Smith's part has thus been needed to make the fragment as sensational as it has been presented in some newspaper articles. We shall return to this problem later on.

Morton Smith is of the opinion that the Greek text is a translation from an Aramaic Gospel also used by Mark. Matthew and Luke may both have known of it, and it has also been known by the editor of the so-called Western text of the synoptic Gospels and the Acts. It would then be extremely ancient Gospel material, although Smith himself reckons the date of the Greek text of the fragment as late as about 125.

This text, however, has an odd feature which Smith never accounts for, and which makes it look so strangely familiar. It seems to have been composed from loose pieces of the Gospels of Mark and John, with some minor fragments from Matthew. Here, all appear in quite different contexts than in the New Testament. In order to judge the matter properly, one should really compare the Greek texts, but many of the similarities are so obvious that they are evident also in a translation into English.

From *The Secret Gospel of Mark* we recognize similar passages in the canonical Gospel of Mark:

Son of David, have mercy on me	Mark 10:47f
the disciples rebuked her	Mark 10:13
Jesus, being angered	Mark 1:41
	(in the "Western" text)
seizing his hand	Mark 1:31
loved him	Mark 10:21
for he was rich	Mark 10:22
a linen cloth over his naked body	Mark 14:51
the mystery of the kingdom of God	Mark 4:11
arising, he returned to the other side of the Jordan	Mark 10:1

The fragment has also several similarities with the Gospel of John, which Smith has been less interested in noting:

she prostrated herself before Jesus	John 11:32
the garden where the tomb was	John 19:41
remained with him that night	John 3:2?
the youth whom Jesus loved	John 13:23 etc.

These similarities have already been discussed in scholarly debate about the letter and its Gospel fragment. They indicate that this is not at all an original Gospel text but a later writing composed by joining material from Mark and John. This is the same kind of reasoning that we have applied to another and far more clumsy composition, *The Gospel of the Holy Twelve*. Morton Smith seems quite alone in his view that the fragment is a piece of genuine Gospel tradition. The date of composition of this "secret Gospel" is, however, a problem. Was it made before the time of Clement, in which case the letter of Clement may be genuine, or were both the letter and the Gospel fragment forged during the period of the early Church, or is this perhaps a modern forgery from a recent century?

It is the last possibility that we will discuss here. This strange splicing of bits and pieces from the Gospels of Mark and John paves the way for the theory that some unknown person with a knowledge of Greek composed the fragments using pieces from two Gospels and perhaps some other pieces from the New Testament. Since all the key words can already be found in the New Testament, it is not really a difficult task to fabricate a text of this kind. What is needed is only a copy of the New Testament in Greek, a concordance, and some patience and knowledge of Greek grammar. It is more difficult to reconstruct a letter by Clement, but there is an extensive Clement index, which provides access to his vocabulary and modes of expression.[131]

The hypothesis that this might be a modern forgery is supported by the fact that expressions which Mark and John use in a natural context, here appear in a way that seems illogical or just odd. We shall look at this a little.

It is said in the story of the rich man (Mark 10:21) that Jesus "loved him," and that is meaningful; it implies that Jesus took an interest in the problem of how a rich man could be saved. In the fragment the same expression appears, but in a different context: the youth, who has just been risen from the dead, "loved" Jesus. This sounds strange, for in our Gospels it is always Jesus who loves other people, never the contrary. Moreover, the word seems strangely inappropriate in this context. Other feelings — amazement or joy at the power of Jesus — might have been expected from someone just risen from the dead.

Still more curious is what follows in the little passage placed separately towards the end. Here the author has changed the relationship, so that the story is now about "the young man whom Jesus loved." The author obviously does not remember what he himself has written, for it was not said that Jesus loved the young man, only that he loved Jesus. What happened here was that the author changed from Mark to John, thus revealing that he knew them both so well that he confused them.

In Mark it is said that the rich man was sorry about Jesus' request of poverty, "for he was rich" (10:22). That again is meaningful. But in the fragment it is said that they came to the young man's house "for he was rich," and that is nonsense. Not only rich people had their own houses in Palestine at the time of Jesus. That was the normal way of living, and what here looks like an explanation is no explanation at all.

Then the youth comes to Jesus "with a linen cloth over his naked body." One may ask why he was attired in this way: Smith suggests that Jesus was going to baptize him, but nothing is said about

it in the fragment, and in the Synoptic tradition there is no indication that Jesus should have baptized.[132] When the same expression
appears in Mark 14:51f, it is used about a young man who gets loose
from the guard in Gethsemane and escapes naked. The meaning
of this episode has often been discussed, but in spite of all obscurities
the external coherence is clear: if somebody is clothed in a linen
cloth only and is deprived of it, he will be naked. In the fragment
the attire of the young man is totally unexplained, and the context
provides no clue.

All these little details together give an impression of unauthen-
ticity. As we have seen, it is unlikely that it conveys a genuine Gospel
tradition. Another oddity is that a Gospel with such insignificant
divergences from the canonical Gospel of Mark should be known
as especially "spiritual" and be surrounded by secrecy. Here no
secrets are revealed at all; we are not even told which secrets about
the Kingdom of God the young man was told by Jesus.

The statement that the Church of Alexandria possessed a secret
Mark tradition about A.D. 200 will also arouse suspicions. Saint
Mark stands as number one in the Alexandrian list of bishops given
by Sextus Julius Africanus (circa A.D. 200). Eusebius of Caesarea
(beginning of the fourth century) also mentions him as the founder
of the Alexandrian Church.[133] Yet the early Alexandrian authors
Clement and Origen never attributed this role to him. If this letter
from Clement were authentic, it would constitute the only evidence
for this tradition in the writings of Clement.

Some of these problems have been taken up in a critical essay
by Quentin Quesnell, in which he requests Smith to clear out some
basic problems before he continues drawing conclusions from the
fragment.[134] Quesnell's starting point is the same book by
Goodspeed about modern apocrypha which we have quoted so often
here. He actualizes Goodspeed's demand that everyone claiming
to have found a new document must present the document itself.
As we have seen, this is just what Notovitch, Ouseley, Szekely, and
others have been unable to do. Nor is Morton Smith able to show
his document: he has not seen the manuscript since 1958, and he
can only present some mediocre photographs, which do not even
cover the entire margins of the manuscript. In spite of his opinion

that the manuscript is sensational, he has made no effort to have it better preserved. He, himself, has acknowledged that books sometimes disappear from libraries.

Quesnell draws the harsh conclusion that the manuscript may be a forgery, made by someone able to write eighteenth-century Greek handwriting, presumably a Greek. He reminds us of the Vinland map in the Yale University Library, which was dated to about 1440, until it was discovered that it had been drawn with an ink that did not exist before 1920. A similar investigation must be done with Smith's manuscript, says Quesnell, before its authenticity may be regarded as certain.

Not even the assurances of linguists make an impression on Quesnell. He notes that Stählin's Clement index was finished in 1936, and that it would be possible to fabricate a new text of Clement with the assistance of this index. The fragment here is fairly brief, and constructing it would not require an immense amount of time.

Quesnell does not make any outright accusations — certainly not against Smith — but he brings our attention to the possibility that this fragment might be the first forgery of a Gospel so skillfully done as to dupe even the specialists. If Smith does obtain the manuscript in the future and does a subject chemical analysis of it, the whole matter may look entirely different.

Morton Smith has made an indignant counterattack, in which he declares that Quesnell accused him of forgery, but I cannot see that he has any reason for this. Whether Quesnell insinuated the charge or whether he quoted Smith carelessly, as claimed, is something that the interested reader will have to consider himself from the original articles. Smith, however, has still said nothing more about the manuscript than what we already know: "I left the MS in the Mar Saba library and have no information as to what has been done with it." In his reply Quesnell again emphasizes the principle that everyone presenting a new document must give his readers a chance to see and investigate the manuscript. This is especially important when the document is presented in a sensational way.

Here stands the controversy about the letter of Clement and the fragment of a secret Gospel of Mark. We cannot advance any further until someone enters the Mar Saba library and produces the manuscript for display to the world.

We now arrive at the second riddle in this matter: how Morton Smith has been able to derive so many strange ideas from this brief and not very disturbing text. He proclaims four theses based on the support of this fragment:

1. that Jesus appeared as a magician;
2. that he baptized himself (not mentioned in the Synoptic Gospels but hinted in John 4:1f);
3. that this baptism in some way put Jesus into a state of ecstasy and gave him an ascension experience;
4. that Jesus was a libertine, who disregarded moral rules and that there were probably elements of homosexuality in his ritual.[135]

The odd thing about Morton Smith's theses is that none of them have any worthwhile support in the fragment. Jesus does make a miracle, but there is nothing more magical about this one than miracles described elsewhere in the Gospels; the baptism is concluded merely from the strange dress of the youth during his visit to Jesus; the third element is completely lacking in the text; and as we have seen, according to the letter, the homosexuality comes only from the falsified additions to the Gospel. If the manuscript were revealed as a forgery, these oddities would be strong indications that Morton Smith is *not* its originator — if, indeed, anyone would believe such a thing. A person who fabricates a text in order to have his favorite ideas confirmed would certainly do it in a more effective way, not making his own arguments more difficult than necessary.

That the four theses are in fact even previously advanced by Morton Smith has been demonstrated by Quesnell and others. Even before 1958, when the discovery was made, Smith had described Jesus as a magician. In addition, the ritual with the ecstatic ascension experience is mentioned by Smith as early as 1941. Genuine or not, the fragment has not brought out any new knowledge of Jesus. It has only been used by Smith as a tool for promoting ideas that existed beforehand in his own head.

15

A Little Test
for the Reader

In order to give the reader a chance to work with textual problems, I here present a document that might be a Gospel fragment unknown until now. The information given here about the manuscript makes no pretense of scholarly veracity. It is the task of the reader to be critical.

The manuscript is said to be a well-preserved papyrus leaf, written in Greek uncial (style of handwriting) on both sides. The leaf can be dated to the first decades of the second century, which implies that it may be contemporary with the famous Papyrus Rylands 457. It is possible that the leaf was discovered in Alexandria toward the end of the 1940s. It is said to have been found among the property left by the Belgian antiquity dealer Albert Eid, who is better known as a former owner of the Coptic manuscript Codex Jung.

This papyrus leaf was bought in 1952 by the Dutch businessman Cornelis van der N. (I here leave out his family name). When he died in 1973, it was inherited by his son, Theodoor van der N. Like his father, he is no papyrologist and does not know Greek at all, but he has reserved for himself the right to have a scholar publish an edition of the manuscript whenever he chooses. For the present, I will only give a preliminary translation of the text.

The literary style of the fragment is close to that of the Synoptic Gospels, and I leave it to the reader to consider whether this may be a Synoptic fragment which was suppressed by the Church during the second century, when the hierarchical order took form. In two passages the text reminds one of Saint Paul rather than of the Synoptics, and I will return to these passages later.

Recto (righthand) page:
His disciples said unto him: "Is it not written about the woman: Your desire shall be for your husband, and he shall rule over you?"

A Little Test for the Reader

(Genesis 3:16). But he answered them: "Verily, verily I say unto you: From the beginning it was not so, before the man and the woman had been tempted by the serpent. Has it not rather been written: Male and female he created them (Genesis 1:27). Thus there is no distinction *(diaphora)* between the man and the woman. I say unto you: Until that day when the Son of Man is revealed, the Gospel shall be preached by women and by men *(hypo gynaikon te kai andron)* from one end of the earth to the other." James answered him and said: "Can it then be lawful for a woman to preach *(keryssein)*." Jesus answered: "O foolish men! Did I not say unto you

Verso (lefthand) page:

that the woman and the man shall have equal part *(meros)* in the Kingdom of God? There shall be neither male nor female *(ouk esto arsen kai thely)*, for you are all the children of your heavenly Father."

In these days a widow approached him and said unto him: "Teacher, what shall I do now, when my son is not willing any more to support *(eparkein)* me?" Jesus said: "The hour has come, when women shall no more be supported by men *(hyp' andron opheleisthai)* but when the woman shall earn her bread by her own work. The work of the man is not more than that of the woman *(Ouk esti to ergon tou andros hyper to tes gynaikos)*. For it is written: If any one will not work, let him not eat. Go, and work with your hands, and be profitable to your neighbor. You shall then no more be anxious, and the Father shall care for you, both now and evermore."

If this text contains a genuine fragment in the Gospel tradition, it is certainly a sensational document, because it deals with the position of the woman more thoroughly and in a far more radical way than the four canonical Gospels or the New Testament in general. But these critical questions follow:
• Is not the topicality of the text an indication that it is not authentic but has been adapted for our time? Or is it possible that it has been suppressed precisely because of its set of values, unacceptable for its own time?
• Is it possible that Jesus could demand of a widow of his time that she begin a manner of life so different from the common one? Or is this a proof of the radicality of Jesus?
• In two passages the text reminds one of the Pauline letters: "There shall be neither male nor female" is almost identical with Galatians 3:28. Can this perhaps be a saying of Jesus hitherto unknown but quoted by Paul?

105

- "If any one will not work, let him not eat" is also a Pauline expression, from 2 Thessalonians 3:10. Is it possible that this is an apocryphal saying, quoted by Jesus as well as by Paul? Jesus says here that "it is written."
- If the text is a genuine Gospel fragment, why does it comprise exactly two complete pericopes (distinct paragraphs)? Is it not more likely that the papyrus leaf would begin and end in the middle of a sentence, as it does in the middle of the text? Or is it likely that a new pericope would begin on a new leaf?
- Is there reason to be skeptical on the grounds that the owner of the manuscript is anonymous and does not give out the original of the text? Or is it better to follow the principle "wait and see"?

As the intelligent reader may have already concluded this is no authentic Gospel fragment but a forgery that I myself made. The inserted Greek words and the solemn language are only there in order to mislead the reader. The papyrus leaf itself and its two Dutch owners are, of course, mere inventions also. The whole thing has only been done as an example of how easily a falsification can be done, and I think, in all modesty, that it is far better done than most of the frauds mentioned in this book. It will not fool a scholar, however; I have tested my forgery on more than one.

I would like to add that my attempt in this criminal genre has not been meant as a contribution to the feminist debate. When I had to choose between various topics of the day, the feminist questions seemed to be the most workable. It is undoubtedly easier to base a believable Gospel text on them than on nuclear power or environmental pollution. I hope, therefore, that no one will feel offended by my choice of an ideological theme.

Conclusion:
A Gospel for Our Time

It is a varying image of Jesus that we have encountered in the many modern apocrypha. Essene brother, traveler to India, vegetarian and friend of animals, nature healer, and magician — there is in fact no limit to the qualities and activities that human imagination has been able to attribute to Jesus. There is, indeed, truth in Albert Schweitzer's famous saying that every time seeks and finds the Jesus that it wants. New times will certainly create new images of Jesus which we cannot yet visualize.

But perhaps it has to be in this way. Is this not one of the remarkable features of Christ, that he can fascinate people in new eras and cultures, that new values can be found in the encounter with him in the Gospels and in the world of imagination?

When I once made a radio talk on modern Jesus legends, I received an interesting letter from a listener in which this very question was raised. The writer asked whether the frailty of Christianity does not depend on its foundation on historical facts. I quote an important passage:

> The need for a religious relevance in the world of today, so lost and inconsistent, cannot be regained only by philological investigations of papyrus scrolls. There is rather a need for a kind of religious creativity, an ability to see what is religiously relevant not only in the form of something different (in ancient documents, or within sophisticated scholarly institutions), but also just in the life we live, at the same time that we betray it by not seeing it, or by not being there except in insufficient measure.[136]

Certainly much modern Bible research has lead to a reification of the faith in Jesus. Everyone who has studied modern exegesis, and has seen how the Gospel is split into ever smaller and more convenient pieces for study by paleography, textual criticism,

107

literary criticism, form criticism, redaction criticism, or whatever it is called, may feel how soon the scent of reality and of divine presence evaporates under clinically scientific procedure. Not least, the school of Bultmann has made Jesus appear very distant, very hypothetical, and difficult to approach. Surely some of the crises of faith in our time have been caused by this way of treating the Gospel.

If scholars today are fragmenting the Gospel and are making the faith in Christ an interesting literary or historical problem, is it then blameworthy if somebody wants to give faith a new life by religious creativity? To create a Gospel for our time, in which Christ speaks to us directly in our present situation, is that not perhaps even laudable? The objection that this would be an inauthentic Gospel is somewhat difficult to uphold, if we consider how the exegetes used to dismiss parts of our canonical Gospels as "congregation theology," "creations by the primitive Church," "secondary insertions," and "redactional framework." If the primitive Church was allowed to make inventions about Jesus within good conscience, why are we forbidden to do it?

Perhaps some unknown authors will create something new about Jesus in the future, and in a form unknown to us. The time of myths is not ended, and perhaps in the future people will be filled with a new Jesus vision that will make our present faith seem powerless and impoverished. The books treated here, however, cannot possibly fulfill that function. Most of them depart from the presupposition that Christianity is a historical religion, and that its writings have to be historical documents. Hence we have all these tricks with lost or hidden papyrus scrolls in Aramaic, Latin, or Pali. The Gospel forgeries are related to the real Gospels just as false coins are to genuine coins: they are unoriginal imitations, more or less well done, and they pretend to be what they are not. Falseness cannot be a road towards creativity.

A reflective reader will also soon be struck by the realization that none of the alleged Gospels gives us a deeper knowledge of Jesus. They do not attribute to him any qualities—divine or human—that might enrich our image of him. On the contrary, we get throughout a superficialized, sentimentalized, and seemingly modern image of Jesus, which some may find attractive for a while, but which will soon reveal its lack of substance. In the long run, most of these apocrypha make exceptionally dull reading.

Say whatever you like about the stories of Jesus in the New Testament—has their freshness, their power, and their ability to move ever been matched? Is it likely that it ever will be?

Notes

1. Edgar J. Goodspeed, *Modern Apocrypha* (Boston: Beacon Press, 1956). An earlier but very similar version of the same book is *Strange New Gospels* (Chicago: University of Chicago Press, 1931).
2. Wolfgang Speyer, *Bücherfunde in der Glaubenswerbung der Antike* (= Hypomnemata 24), Göttingen 1970.
3. The most recent edition is Edgar Hennecke's *New Testament Apocrypha*, vols. 1 and 2, ed. Wilhelm Schneemelcher, English trans. ed. R. McL. Wilson (Philadelphia: Westminster Press, 1965). Montague Rhodes James, *The Apocryphal New Testament* (Oxford University Press, 1924), is still very useful and sometimes includes material omitted by Hennecke and Schneemelcher.
4. For *The Letter of Abgarus* and the answer by Jesus, see Hennecke and Schneemelcher, vol. 1 p. 433 f.; James, p. 476 f. The most extensive treatment of the letter is in Ernst von Dobschütz, *Christusbilder* (= Texte und Untersuchungen NF 3), Leipzig 1899, pp. 102–196, 158 +–249 +, 29 + +–156 + + .
5. *Apocalypse of Paul:* Quotation from Hennecke and Schneemelcher, vol. 2, p. 759 f. *Sozomens:* Ibid., p. 755.
6. *Pseudepigraphy and forgery:* The recent literature on this subject is most extensive. I will mention some of the more important works: Wolfgang Speyer, "Religiöse Pseudepigraphie and literarische Fälschung im Altertum," *Jahrbuch für Antike und Christentum* 8/9 (1965–66), pp. 88–125. Idem, art. Fälschung. literarische, *Reallexikon für Antike und Christentum* 7 (1967), pp. 235–277. Idem, "Angebliche Übersetzungen des heidnischen und christlichen Altertums," *Jahrbuch für Antike und Christentum* 11/12 (1968/69), pp. 26–41. Idem, *Bücherfunde in der Glaubenswerbung der Antike* (= Hypomnemata 24), Göttingen 1970. Idem, *Die literarische Fälschung im heidnischen und jüdischen Altertum* (= Handbuch der Altertumswissenschaft 1:2), Munich 1971. Norbert Brox, *Falsche Verfasserangaben, Zur Erklärung der frühchristlichen Pseudepigraphie* (= Stuttgarter Bibel-Studien 79), Stuttgart 1975. Idem, ed., *Pseudepigraphie in der heidnischen und jüdisch-christlichen Antike* (= Wege der Forschung 184), Wissenschaftliche Buchgesellschaft, Darmstadt 1977. Kurt von Fritz, ed., *Pseudepigrapha I* (= Entretiens sur l'antiquité classique 18), Vandoeuvres-Geneva 1972.
7. *The Letter of Lentulus* is a fairly late apocryphon, probably from

the thirteenth century. It is not mentioned by Hennecke and Schneemelcher, but James gives a common form of the text, p. 477 f. The various versions have been edited and commented by von Dobschütz, pp. 293++–330++. Goodspeed has a short chapter on the letter in his *Modern Apocrypha*, pp. 88–91. *The Letter of Lentulus* describes Jesus in a way well known to us from Christian art; his hair is brown with long, curling locks and is parted in the middle of the head, and his beard is a little forked. This writing purports to have been made by a Roman named Lentulus, who is said to have served in Judea in the time of Jesus. He cannot be identified as an historical person.

8. A curious example of the way in which the alleged discovery of a book may be used as a theme in a modern novel is James Hall Roberts, *The Q Document* (New York: William Morrow, 1964). It has no great literary merit but is interesting precisely because of its theme: an alleged manuscript collection from early Christian times is found in Japan, *inter alia* with an autography by Jesus, but the whole lot is shown to be a forgery. The author has a certain knowledge of the problems and once mentions *The Essene Letter* (p. 238 f.).

9. *The Latin Infancy Gospel: L'évangile de la jeunesse de Notre-Seigneur Jésus-Christ, d'après S. Pierre*, Latin text and French translation by Catulle Mendès (Armand Collin, 1894). See James, p. 89. *The Gospel of Josephus:* Goodspeed, *Modern Apocrypha*, pp. 76–80.

10. *Oahspe:* See Goodspeed, *Modern Apocrypha*, pp. 102–105. *Similar books:* Geraldine Cummins, *The Scripts of Cleophas*, (London: Rider & Co., 1928). The books *The Testament of Love* and *My Son* (the latter by the Blessed Virgin) were published by the Lord Mikaals Centre, of The Aetherius Society.

11. *The Gospel of Barnabas:* The first edition is *The Gospel of Barnabas*, edited and translated from the Italian manuscript in the Imperial Library at Vienna by Lonsdale and Laura Ragg (Oxford: Clarendon Press, 1907). I have used a modern Muslim edition of the same, published by Begum Aisha Bawany Waqf, (Karachi, n.d.). The most modern and extensive work on *The Gospel of Barnabas* is *Evangile de Barnabé*, Recherches sur la composition et l'origine par Luigi Cirillo; traduction et notes par Luigi Cirillo et Michel Frémeaux; préface d'Henry Corbin, Paris 1977. The Spanish version was long believed to be lost, but an incomplete copy was discovered in Australia. See J. E. Fletcher, "The Spanish Gospel of Barnabas," *Novum Testamentum* 18:4 (1976), pp. 314–320. The Spanish text of the story mentioned is printed in Fletcher, p. 320.

12. For Ahmad's use of *The Gospel of Barnabas*, see pp. 63–64.

13. *The Death Warrant of Jesus:* I have not been able to find out in which issue of *Le Droit* this document first appeared. The entire article with the text of the death warrant was reprinted in *Le Moniteur Universel*, 4 May 1839 (p. 644), where it is said to have been published recently *(dernièrement)* in *Le Droit*, and where the notice in the *Gazette de France*

is also mentioned. A second article by Isambert followed on May 13 (p. 702) with further critical comments, which still retain their validity. The French leaflets are entitled *Sentence rendue par Ponce Pilate, Gouverneur (-regent) de la Basse Galilée, portant que Jésus de Nazareth subira la peine (le supplice) de la croix.* I have seen three such prints: a broadsheet, printed in Paris in 1858, by Bonaventure & Ducessois; a leaflet published together with a Way of the Cross (and with ecclesiastical approbation!), Paris 1866 by A. Liébert Cic; another broadsheet without date, printed in Cayes by C. A. Lhérison.

The German version is a translation from *Le Droit* and was first published in *Kölnische Zeitung*, 25 September 1849 (dated September 22), by a Dr. Thesmar. It has been reprinted in Rudolf Hofmann, *Das Leben Jesu nach den Apokryphen* (Leipzig: 1851), pp. 366–368, and is said to have been taken from *Neue Preussische Zeitung*, September 28. Hofmann's text contains several errors: the year 1280 has become 1820, and the sentence in which Jesus is accused of calling himself Son of God has been omitted.

The American versions are described by Goodspeed in *Modern Apocrypha*, pp. 92–96. I have only seen one modern edition in *The Crucifixion by an Eye-Witness*, Indian reprint of the Chicago edition from 1907, (see below, Note 48). It was included in William Overton Clough's *Gesta Pilati* (see below, Note 64), which I have only seen in a Swedish translation from 1886.

14. *The earlier history of the death warrant* is thoroughly told in an article by Rudolf Berliner, "Das Urteil des Pilatus," *Die Christliche Kunst* 30 (1933–34), pp. 128–147. *The learned discussion about the sentence of Pilate:* Berliner, pp. 128–132. The most important apocryphon in the debate was *The Gospel of Nicodemus.* An undefined apocryphal version of Pilate's verdict was presented by Paul of Middleburg (Semproniensis), Berliner, p. 133 f.

15. *The Vienne document:* Berliner, pp. 132–136. The alleged find was published in a book from the beginning of the sixteenth century, *Vie de Jésus-Christ avec sa Passion.* On this book, see J. P. Migne, *Encyclopédie théologique* 14 (Dictionnaire des légendes), Paris 1955, col. 1092 ff. (by Comte de Douhet). Quoted by Hofmann, p. 366, Berliner, p. 132. *The Latin text* is not known from the sixteenth century, but there is a Latin version printed on an English broadsheet from the nineteenth century: *The Sentence of Condemnation as passed by Pontius Pilate against the Lord Jesus Christ, the Saviour of the World.* From an early manuscript in the possession of Mr. C. Havell, Reading, printed in 1851. It has both the Latin text and an English translation.

16. *The earlier Aquila sentence:* Berliner, pp. 136–141. The original Italian text (according to Borello) is printed in Berliner, pp. 138 and 140. An Italian manuscript from the seventeenth century, in the Spanish State Archives of Simancas, is printed in Aurelio de Santos Otero, *Los Evangelios*

Apocrifos, 2nd ed., (Madrid: La Editorial Catolica, 1963), pp. 532–535.
It is evidently the same text but here in a corrupt form. A Spanish transla-
tion of this document was further translated into French by a certain M.
Lacaze, and was published with the title *Sentence prononcée par Ponce-
Pilate contre Jésus-Christ le 25 mars de l'an 73 de l'étasblissement de
l'Empire romain,* with an introduction by a M. Jaybert, Toulouse 1872.
The original Italian version is treated in two works to which I have not
had access: G. Pansa, *Miti, leggende e superstizioni dell'Abruzzo,* vol. 2,
Sulmona 1927; and E. F. Sutcliffe, "An Apocryphal Form of Pilate's Verdict," *The Catholic Biblical Quarterly* 9 (1947), pp. 436–441 (mentioned
by de Santos Otero).

17. *The French translation* has the title *Thrésor admirable de la sentence
prononcée par Ponce Pilate contre nostre Sauveur Jésus-Christ,* printed
by Guillaume Julien, Paris 1581. See Berliner, p. 136. It was reprinted
by S. Le Febvre, Paris 1621. A third edition appeared in 1839, printed
by J. Techener. It seems to have been edited by a certain Augustin Soulié
as a move against Isambert's criticism of the article in *Le Droit.* The editor
does not seem to have observed the difference between the parchment and
the copperplate versions.

18. *German prints:* Berliner mentions one from Nürnberg 1581, one from
Regensburg (the same year), and a reprint from Magdeburg 1584, see footnote p. 142. *The Spanish translation* had a great impact at court and among
the people according to a vivid account by Fray Rodrigo de Yepes, *Trac-
tado . . . de la tierra . . . de Palestina,* Madrid 1583. Berliner, p. 138.
Fray Rodrigo is unjustly accused of originating the Aquila sentence by P.
R. Lyell, *The Sentence of Pontius Pilate, being an alleged copy of the formal judgment against Jesus* (London: 1922). Another Spanish translation
was made in 1786 by the Bishop of Seville, D. N. Guerra. Its text is printed
in de Santos Otero, *Los Evangelios Apocrifos,* pp. 532–535 (in parallel with
the Italian text).

19. *The disappearance of the older Aquila sentence:* It is of course possible
that there have been later prints, which have now been forgotten. I have
seen a Greek print from about 1940: *Ison tēs kata tou Sotēros Iēsou Christou
. . . apofaseōs,* published in one volume with the prophecies of Hieronymos
Agathangelos, an apocryphon that we will not discuss here.

20. *Denon:* Some more recent books are: J. Nowinski, *Baron Dominique
Vivant Denon* (Rutherford, New Jersey: Fairleigh Dickinson University
Press, 1970); and J. Chatelain, *Dominique-Vivant Denon et le Louvre de
Napoléon* (Paris: Librairie académique Perrin, 1973). *The sale of Denon's
cabinet:* See *British Museum General Catalogue,* vol. 51, col. 190 f.

21. *The Protocol of the Sanhedrin:* The earliest prints are listed by
Berliner, p. 141 ff. The protocol is printed together with the Aquila sentence
in the oldest German editions (see above, Note 18). Leaflets from Augsburg
show the protocol in combination with the Vienne sentence. See Berliner,
p. 142 and note 2. I do not know anything about possible English or

American editions.

22. *Letters from heaven:* Goodspeed presented and compared three such letters in the *Anglican Theological Review*, vol. 15 (1933), and has a chapter about them in his *Modern Apocrypha*, pp. 70–75. Their origin is demonstrated in Robert Priebsch's posthumous work *Letter from Heaven on the Observance of the Lord's Day*, Medium Aevum 5, supplementary volume, Oxford 1936. There are several German works on the letters from heaven: a huge edition of various versions is M. Bittner, *Der vom Himmel gefallene Brief Christi* (= Denkschriften der Kaiserlichen Akademie der Wissenschaften, Phil.-hist Kl., vol. 51:1), Vienna 1906. A good survey is Rudolf Stübe, *Der Himmelsbrief*, Tübingen 1918. Also see Speyer, *Bücherfunde*, pp. 23–42.

23. *Letters used as amulets:* Stübe, pp. 1–4.

24. *The letter from Ibiza:* The Latin text is edited in Priebsch, p. 1 f. See Stübe, p. 12 f., and Goodspeed, *Modern Apocrypha*, p. 72. Aurelio de Santos Otero, Der apokryphe sogenannte Sonntagsbrief, *Studia Patristica*, vol. 3.1 (= Texte und Untersuchungen, vol. 78), Berlin 1961, pp. 290–296. Speyer, *Bücherfunde*, p. 27 ff.

25. *Jewish influence in France:* Priebsch, p. 27. There was a Jewish influence of the same kind in Spain, de Santos Otero, p. 295 f. *Synods about the Sunday observance:* Priebsch, p. 7 f. *Letter on Iceland:* Priebsch, p. 14. The letter is mentioned in the so-called Leidarvisa from about 1200, Priebsch, p. 15 f.

26. *French or Spanish origin:* This is Priebsch's and Stübe's opinion. But the origin is still obscure, for de Santos Otero has been able to demonstrate Byzantine elements in letters from heaven in the West, p. 292. (Unfortunately he did not know of Priebsch's work.) The cultural contacts between Byzantium and southern France were strong in the Merovingian Age, and the answer to the priority concerning the letters from heaven cannot be ascertained without further research. *Later uses of letters from heaven in millenarist and revolutionary movements:* Norman Cohn, *The Pursuit of the Millennium* (London: Paladin, 1970), pp. 62, 94f, 129–132, and *passim*.

27. *The heavenly book:* Stübe, pp. 28-43. Speyer, pp. 23–42.

28. *Mormonism:* I have mainly used three American works: William A. Linn, *The Story of the Mormons* (New York, 1902); I. Woodbridge Riley, *The Founder of Mormonism, a psychological study of Joseph Smith, Jr.* (New York, 1902); Fawn M. Brodie, *No man knows my history* (New York: Alfred Knopf, 1946). All these books take a critical attitude (Brodie was an ex-Mormon and therefore biased), but I have found no reason to doubt the documents quoted, on which I base my personal judgment.

29. *The revelation of the Book of Mormon:* Smith told the story himself in his *History of Joseph Smith, the Prophet, by Himself* (Salt Lake City, 1902). Extracts from this huge work about the main events are easily available from the Mormon Church.

30. *Anachronisms:* Ether 9:18 f., 1 Nephi 18:25, 1 Nephi 4:9. All these are mentioned by Linn, p. 97.

31. *Anti-Catholic elements:* 1 Nephi 13:4-9, 14:3-17, mentioned by Brodie, p. 59 f. *Freemasons:* Helaman 6:18-23, Brodie, p. 65, cf. p. 279 ff. Some of the secret rituals of the Mormons seem to be inspired by the Freemasons.

32. *Lehi's dream:* 1 Nephi 8:2-35. The elder Joseph Smith's dream is retold by Lucy Smith in her *Biographical Sketches of Joseph Smith the Prophet and His Progenitors for Many Generations* (Liverpool, 1853), p. 58 f. Both dreams are printed in parallels in Riley, pp. 114-117. Shorter quotations in Brodie, p. 58 f.

33. *The "Egyptian" script:* Smith's own sample of "Caractors" is shown in facsimile in Riley, plate at p. 81; Linn, plate at p. 40; Brodie, plate at p. 51. Martin Harris made a trip to New York and showed some proofs of the script to Professor Charles Anthon at Columbia College, who could not read ancient Egyptian either. After his return, Harris reported that Anthon had stated that the script was Egyptian but that he had torn his own statement into pieces, when he heard that the book had been revealed by an angel. Harris' record is printed in *The Pearl of Great Price;* cf. Riley, p. 83, note. Anthon rejected this story in a letter, dated Feb. 17, 1834; printed in Linn, p. 39. He stated in his letter that it contained all kinds of signs but no Egyptian ones. The letter is interesting, as it confirms some accounts about the translation, mentioned in this chapter.

34. *The Spaulding-Rigdon theory:* Linn accepts the theory, pp. 50-73, but it is rejected by Riley, pp. 369-396, and by Brodie, pp. 419-433. Riley demonstrates convincingly that Rigdon cannot have transmitted the *Book of Mormon* to Smith at this time. Also see Brodie, p. 428 ff. The Spaulding theory was revived in 1977 and got some publicity in the American press. Howard Doulder, an expert on handwriting, had studied a manuscript by Spaulding and an early manuscript of the *Book of Mormon*, and believed that he could prove that both documents were written by the same hand. But he later retracted his declaration, as did his supporter, Henry Silver. The Mormon Church issued an official refutation of Doulder's statements (August 1977), which also contained a comparison between proofs of handwriting. *Fate* 31:4 (1978) pp. 10-16.

35. *Ethan Smith:* Riley, pp. 122-128; Brodie, p. 46 f. The idea that the American Indians might be descendants of the ten lost tribes of Israel was already held by some of the first Spanish conquerors. In England it seems to have been expressed for the first time by Thomas Thorowgood in 1650. I have not delved any deeper into this problem. Some references are to be found in James Webb, *The Occult Underground* (La Salle, Illinois: Open Court Publishing Company, 1974), p. 148, note 23.

36. *An Indian origin of the story:* See Åke V. Ström, "Red Indian Elements in Early Mormonism," *Temenos* 5 (1969) pp. 120-168. About Walam Olum, see especially pp. 132-134. The authenticity of Walam

Olum, however, is denied by some scholars, and is also mentioned by Ström p. 133. The similarity between American Indian cultural heroes and Jesus has been shown in a suggestive but weakly documented book, L. Taylor Hansen, *He Walked the Americas* (London: Neville Spearman, 1963). An investigation would probably show that the motif of "Jesus in America" is as fruitful as that of "Jesus in India."

37. *The fragment by Saint John:* According to Brodie, p. 96, the "fragment" originally consisted of three verses only, and was printed in this form in the *Book of Commandments*, the first edition of Smith's revelations (apart from the *Book of Mormon*). It was printed in Jackson, Missouri, 1833. In the present official collection, *Doctrine and Covenants of the Church of the Latter-Day Saints*, first printed in Kirtland, Ohio, 1835, the fragment has eight verses.

38. *Emma Smith about the plates:* Account in *Saints Herald* 26 (1879) p. 289 according to Brodie, p. 42 f.

39. *Harris as a secretary:* Linn, p. 37 f; Brodie, p. 53 f. *David Whitmer's account:* Linn, p. 42; Brodie, p. 60 f.

40. *The testimony of the eight:* Hiram Page, the only witness who did not bear the name of Whitmer or Smith, had married into the Whitmer family. Brodie, p. 79.

41. *The three witnesses: History of Joseph Smith.*

42. *The apostasy of Cowdery and Harris:* Linn, pp. 81–85.

43. *Joseph Smith as a money-digger:* Linn, pp. 15–22; Brodie, pp. 19–21, 30 f. *The court protocol* was rediscovered and published in 1883; it is reprinted in its entirety in Brodie, pp. 405–407.

44. *Smith's revised Bible* has been very little known outside The Reorganized Church and is not mentioned by Riley or Linn (the latter unfortunately refers to the *Book of Mormon* as "the Mormon Bible"). Brodie, p. 116 f. I have used the twentieth edition, printed in Lamoni, Iowa, 1920.

45. *The Book of Abraham:* Linn, pp. 139–141; Brodie, pp. 170–173. *The Pearl of Great Price* was not published until after Smith's death, in Liverpool, 1851. Apart from the *Book of Abraham* it also contains the *Book of Moses*, received by Smith as a direct revelation. Various criticisms by Egyptologists are collected in *Joseph Smith, Jr., as a Translator*, by F. S. Spalding (earlier bishop of the Protestant Episcopal Church) (Salt Lake City, 1912). There is a great deal of fresh evidence in a long series of articles in *The Improvement Era*, vol. 71–72 (1968–69), under the rubric "A New Look at the Pearl of Great Price," by Dr. Hugh Nibley, who is Professor of History and Religion at Brigham Young University, Salt Lake City. Nibley deals with the debate of 1912, but has also studied the original manuscripts and has been able to demonstrate a certain carelessness by some Egyptologists in writing about Smith's papyri. The same question has also been treated by Nibley and by the Egyptologist John A. Wilson in *Dialogue 3* (1968). (*Dialogue* is the scientific periodical of Brigham Young University.)

46. *Genuine pseudepigraphy:* Speyer, *Bücherfunde*, p. 107 f. Also see Norbert Brox's review of this book in *Jahrbuch für Antike und Christentum* 13 (1970) p. 101 f., where Speyer's opinion is criticized. *The Book of Mormon as a "Targum":* Krister Stendahl, The Sermon on the Mount and Third Nephi, in *Reflections on Mormonism, Judaeo-Christian Parallels*, ed. Truman G. Madsen (Provo, Utah: Religious Study Center, Brigham Young University, 1978).

47. *Automatic writing:* Riley, p. 195 f., where the problem is discussed.

48. *The American versions of the Essene Letter* are discussed in Goodspeed, *Modern Apocrypha*, p. 21, note 2, but his representation of them is inexact and in need of some explanation. The earliest edition now extant is *The Crucifixion by an Eye-Witness*, Supplemental Harmonic Series, vol. 2 (Chicago: Indo-American Book Co., 1907). The second edition (also from 1907) is still being reprinted by the Ahmadiyya movement; I have used an edition printed by Syed Abdul Hayee, Lahore, 1977. It also contains a translation of *The Letter of Lentulus* and of *The Death Warrant of Jesus Christ* (in the copperplate version). An older edition is said to have existed, printed in 1873; by whom and where is unknown. The editor of the 1907 edition ("T. K.") states that it was made by a German in poor English, which is why he revised it. At the turn of the century, only a single copy remained of this earliest edition, of which we have heard nothing more. The next American translation is *The Crucifixion and the Resurrection of Jesus, by an Eye-Witness* (Los Angeles: Holmes Book Company, 1919). According to Goodspeed, it was translated from the second Swedish edition (Köping, 1880). A copy of the Swedish translation had come into the possession of The Theosophical Society of Muskegon, Michigan, and somebody made a translation of it into English, which was found in 1904. These two American editions thus seem to be independent, but the similarity of the titles suggests some relationship. The latest edition I know of is called *An Eye Witness Account;* it was published by The Academy of Mystic Arts, New York, 1975, and has a foreword by somebody with the exotic title of Grand Master, BLANA MED PA, Grand Master Temple of the White Flame. How this limited edition is related to the others is unknown to me. Nor do I know what kind of Freemasonry is practiced by the Grand Master Temple of the White Flame.

49. The original German edition is *Wichtige Enthüllungen über die wirkliche Todesart Jesu*, printed by Chr. Ernst Kollmann, Leipzig 1849. The second book, about the birth and childhood of Jesus, is *Historische Enthüllungen über die wirklichen Ereignisse der Geburt und Jugend Jesu*, also printed by Kollmann in 1849.

50. *The Essenes:* A good summary of what was known about them before the find of the Dead Sea Scrolls is found in Emil Schürer, *History of the Jewish People in the Time of Jesus* (London: Hamish Hamilton, 1890), pp. 188–218. The early debate about the Dead Sea Scrolls and the Essenes is related at length in Millar Burrows, *The Dead Sea Scrolls* (London: Secker

& Warburg, 1956), pp. 279–296; and idem., *More Light on the Dead Sea Scrolls* (London: Secker & Warburg, 1958), pp. 263–274. Since then the discussion has continued, but there is no real reason to question the general view of Burrows. Today there are few who deny any relationship between the Qumran sect and the Essenes.

51. *The white robes:* Josephus, *The Jewish War* II.8.3, 5, 7. *The herbs: The Jewish War* II.8.6.

52. *Johann Nepomuk Truelle:* I have not seen either of his two books against *The Essene Letter*. They are *Die wichtigen historischen Enthüllungen über Geburt und Todesart Jesu (bei Chr. Ernst Kollmann) sind ein literarischer Betrug,* Regensburg 1849; and *Für jeden Christen höchst notwendige Aufklärungen über die allein wahre Todesart Jesu Christi,* Regensburg 1850, both printed by Manz.

53. *The early Essene romanticism:* See Burrows, *More Light,* pp. 76–78.

54. *Hermann Samuel Reimarus:* See Albert Schweitzer, *The Quest of the Historical Jesus* (first printed in 1906), pp. 13–26 (originally published in German with the title *Von Reimarus zu Wrede*). Reimarus died in 1768, but his hypotheses were not published until 1774–1777 by G. E. Lessing. They were printed anonymously with the title *Wolffenbüttler Fragmente eines Ungenannten,* and are still generally referred to as "the Wolffenbüttel Fragments."

55. Karl Friedrich Bahrdt, *Briefe über die Bibel im Volkston, Eine Wochenschrift von einem Prediger auf dem Lande* (Halle, 1782). See Schweitzer, pp. 38–44.

56. Karl Heinrich Venturini, *Natürliche Geschichte des grossen Propheten von Nazareth,* vol. 1–4, Ägypten & Bethlehem (= Copenhagen) 1800–1802. See Schweitzer, pp. 44–48. Schweitzer points out that Venturini's novel is the immediate model of *The Essene Letter,* pp. 162 ff., but does not mention Truelle, who originally discovered the connection between the "Letter" and the novel.

57. *The radicalism of the 1840s* is extensively described in Carl Mirbt, art. Lichtfreunde, in *Realencyklopädie für protestantische Theologie und Kirche,* vol. 11, Leipzig 1902, pp. 465–474.

58. *The debate about The Essene Letter:* Regarding Truelle's pamphlet, see Note 52. A certain Dr. Johann Friedrich Wohlfarth published a pamphlet in the same year with the title *Würdigung und Beleuchtung einer soeben bei Kollmann in Leipzig unter dem Titel: "Enthüllungen über die wirkliche Todesart Jesu" erschienenen Schrift,* Weimar, 1849, printed by Voigt. The critics were answered by the anonymous editor in two pamphlets: *Jesus der Essäer, oder, Die Religion der Zukunft,* with the subtitle: *Eine Beleuchtung der "Enthüllungen, über die wirkliche Todesart Jesu," Verbunden mit einer Kritik der Einwendungen der orthodoxen Theologie, wie sie die Schrift des F. S. Kirchenraths Dr. Wohlfarth ausspricht,* Leipzig, 1849, printed by Chr. Ernst Kollmann, and *Die Enthüllungen, im Kampfe mit der protestantischen und katholischen Orthodoxie,*

Controverspredigt gegen Hrn. Nep: Truelle, seine letzte Schrift und Seines Gleichen, Leipzig 1859, printed by Kollmann. It is typical that the controversy between "religious freedom" and "orthodoxy" obscured the question of authenticity.

59. *Masonic rituals:* In the description of the initiation there is also a reminiscence from Josephus, who states that the Essene novices were given a hatchet, a girdle, and a white garment (*The Jewish War* II.8.7). The hatchet was used for digging a pit for their private needs (II.8.9). Also see the most recent edition of *The Essene Letter* by a Masonic lodge, Note 48 above.

60. *Swedish editions:* Stockholm 1951, Köping 1880, Malmö 1926, Uddevalla 1977. *French edition: Le mort de Jésus*, Paris 1963. See Goodspeed, *Modern Apocrypha*, p. 21, note 2. *The translation into Urdu* was made by Mian Mirajuddin, *Waqia Salib-i-Masih ki Chasmdid Shahadat* (Lahore: n.d.).

61. *Recent hypotheses about the Essenes:* See Burrows, *More Light*, ch. 23. The idea that Jesus himself had been an Essene was championed by A. Powell Davies, *The Meaning of the Dead Sea Scrolls* (New York: Mentor Books, 1956). This is a most dubious work from a scholarly point of view and has now disappeared from the debate. Cf. Burrows, *More Light*, pp. 77–82. *John the Baptist as an Essene:* See Burrows, *More Light*, ch. 5.

62. *The letter from Pilate:* In Andreas Faber-Kaiser, *Jesus Died in Kashmir* (London: Gordon & Cremonesi, 1978); paperback edition (London: Abacus Books, 1978), pp. 22–24. The references here are to the paperback edition.

63. *Acts of Pilate:* See Hennecke and Schneemelcher, vol. 2, pp. 444–484.

64. *Mahan's "find"* was first published with the title *A Correct Transcript of Pilate's Court*, 1879. The following year it was reprinted at Shelbyville, Indiana, with a long introduction and notes by the Reverend George Sluter, who called it *The Acta Pilati*. In 1880 it was published for the first time by William Overton Clough in his collection *Gesta Pilati*, printed at Indianapolis. There is a Swedish translation of this book, printed in Köping in 1886; this is, in fact, the only version I have seen. The history of the early editions is told by Goodspeed, pp. 28–31.

65. *Joseph Méry:* The story *Ponce Pilate à Vienne* was printed in *Revue de Paris*, Jan. 1837, pp. 193–212. It is signed "Méry" without any Christian name, according to a common French usage, but I take for granted that it was Joseph Méry who was the author. At the same time he published a number of short stories in Paris. *The Italian translation* is *Ponzio Pilato a Vienna*, Milan 1837; *the Spanish translation* is similarly entitled *Poncio Pilato en Vienna*, Bogotá 1838; in both the author is indicated as "Méry." *The American translation*, however, gives no author but is said to be "extracted from an old Latin manuscript recently found at Vienne"; its title is *Pontius Pilate's Account of the Condemnation of Jesus Christ*

and his own Mental Sufferings, Boston 1842. Regarding this version, see Goodspeed, pp. 42, 48. *An Arabian translation* was made by an Orthodox bishop, Jerasimus Jared, and was published in 1889. An English translation of this translation was published by B. Shehadi in New South Wales, Australia, in 1893, and was in turn reprinted in East Orange, New Jersey, in 1917. The publication histories of this kind of apocrypha may sometimes be indescribably complicated. See Goodspeed, pp. 46–49.

66. *Anatole France:* See Goodspeed, pp. 42, 48. The short story "Le Procurateur de Judée," first published in *Le Temps* on Christmas Day in 1889, was later included in the collection *L'étui de nacre* (1891). Méry's story is not indicated as a source for Anatole France in B. M. Woodbridge, "The Original Inspiration of Le Procurateur de Judée," *Modern Language Notes*, no. 40 (1925), pp. 483–485.

67. *The Archko Volume:* The story here follows Goodspeed, pp. 33–44.

68. Among the modern Acts of Pilate is also the curious *Letters of Pontius Pilate, written during his Governorship of Judaea to his friend Seneca in Rome*, ed. W. P. Crozier (London: Jonathan Cape, 1928). In this case it is possible that the author meant them to be understood as a fiction. He does not relate any story of a book find but asks the reader to decide whether they are authentic. From a literary point of view, the "letters" seem void of interest.

69. Nicolas Notovitch, *La vie inconnue de Jésus-Christ*, first published by Paul Ollendorf, Paris 1894. Within a short time three English translations were published: *The Unknown Life of Jesus Christ*, trans. J. H. Connelly and L. Landsberg (New York: G. W. Dillingham, 1894); *The Unknown Life of Jesus Christ*, trans. Alexina Loranger (Chicago, New York: Rand, McNally & Co., 1894); *The Unknown Life of Christ*, trans. Violet Crispe (London: Hutchinson, 1895). Italian and German translations appeared in 1894, a Swedish translation in 1896, and a Spanish version in 1909. See Goodspeed, p. 3 f.

70. *Notovitch's story about his "find":* He first refers to the manuscripts as "scrolls" *(rouleaux)*, but later describes them as "two thick bound books" *(deux gros livres cartonnés)*. But Tibetan books are neither scrolls nor bound in our way. They consist of oblong leaves, imitating palm leaves; they are kept loose between wooden plates, and the whole is kept wrapped in a piece of cloth.

71. Max Müller's article, "The Alleged Sojourn of Christ in India," was published in *The Nineteenth Century*, vol. 36 (1894), pp. 515–522.

72. J. Archibald Douglas, "The Chief Lama of Hemis on the Alleged Unknown Life of Christ," *The Nineteenth Century*, vol. 39 (1896), pp. 667–678. It has never been clear which interpreter Notovitch might have used, if he had one at all. The inhabitants who could interpret between English or Urdu and Tibetan were so few that it was easy to question them all, and no one seems to have been Notovitch's interpreter. The lama himself stated that he did not speak English or Urdu.

73. *Madame Blavatsky:* It has been suggested that she originated the idea of the hidden Tibetan manuscript. Her last great work, *The Secret Doctrine*, 1st ed., 1888, contains passages from a book named *The Book of Dzyan*, which she claimed was the oldest manuscript in the world, kept by the mahatmas in a hidden valley somewhere in the Himalayas. There are indications, however, that her quotations were taken from a far later work, the medieval Kabbalistic tract *Sifra Di-Tseniutha;* she might have known it from Christian Knorr von Rosenroth's *Kabbala Denudata* (1677–84), for this book contains a Latin translation of the Hebrew text. See Gershom Scholem, *Major Trends in Jewish Mysticism* (New York: Schocken paperback ed., 1961), p. 398f. Scholem points out that Madame Blavatsky mentions this tract in her earlier work *Isis Unveiled*, and calls it *Siphra Dzeniuta;* from this he draws the reasonable conclusion that the name *Dzyan* (not in *Isis Unveiled*) is in fact derived from *Dzeniuta*. Madame Blavatsky herself derives the name from the two unrelated Sanskrit words *dhyana* and *jñana*. A discussion of her manipulations with texts and languages, however, is beside the scope of this book. I willingly admit that I have not delved into this problem more deeply, and that Scholem may be mistaken.

74. *The Buddhist origin of Christianity:* It is not clear what might be the direct source of inspiration for Notovitch. Arthur Lillie wrote a number of books on this subject: *Buddhism in Christendom, or Jesus, the Essene* . . . (London: Kegan Paul & Co., 1887); *The Influence of Buddhism on Primitive Christianity* (London: Sonnenschein & Co., 1893); *India in Primitive Christianity* (London: Kegan Paul & Co., 1909). Lillie is known to have inspired *The Gospel of the Holy Twelve*. The German professor Rudolf Seydel of Leipzig had similar ideas: *Das Evangelium von Jesu in seinen Verhältnissen zu Buddha-Sage und Buddha-Lehre mit fortlaufender Rücksicht auf andere Religionskreise*, Leipzig 1882; *Buddha und Christus*, Breslau 1884; *Die Buddha-Legende und das Leben Jesu nach den Evangelien*, 2nd ed., Weimar 1897.

75. *Notovitch's followers:* Regarding the new edition of 1926, see Goodspeed, p. 14. Nicholas Roerich described his travels in *Altai-Himalaya, A Travel Diary* (London: Jarrolds, 1930), see especially pp. 89–94, 114, 118 f. His son, George N. Roerich, described the same travels in his book *Trails to Inmost Asia* (New Haven: Yale University Press, 1931), where Hemis is also mentioned (pp. 20, 27, 30) but not Notovitch or his manuscript.

76. *Ahmadiyya:* See the informative article by Wilfred Cantwell Smith, "Ahmadiyya," *Encyclopedia of Islam*, 2nd ed. (London: Leiden & Co., 1960), pp. 301–303.

77. *The Legend of Ahmadiyya* which tells how Jesus survived the crucifixion, fled to India, and died there, is spread over the world by missionaries of the movement and their publications. As far as I know, the only book written about this legend from an historical and critical point

of view is a short one which I published in Swedish with the title *Jesus i Kashmir* (Stockholm: Proprius, 1981). The reader may have to resort to the books of the Ahmadiyya movement with all their misunderstandings and grave inaccuracies. Ahmad's own point of view is propounded in *Jesus in India* (Rabwah, W. Pakistan: The Ahmadiyya Muslim Foreign Missions Department, n.d. preface 1962). It was first published in Urdu in 1899 with the title *Masih Hindustan mein*. Ahmad is said to have developed his arguments in a book written in Arabic with the title *Al-Huda* (1902); I have not had access to it. His arguments have been carried on by his disciples; cf. the following footnote. A congress on this topic was held in London in June 1978, and the papers read there have been published in *Truth about the Crucifixion* (London: The London Mosque, 1978). The papers discuss various hypotheses on the survival of Jesus as well as on his alleged travels to Kashmir. There are also a few Westerners who have been inspired by the legend, such as Andreas Faber-Kaiser, *Jesus Died in Kashmir*. He accepts the legend without reserve without being a formal member of the Ahmadiyya movement.

78. *The Gospel of Barnabas:* See Ahmad, *Jesus in India*, p. 26. *The Essene Letter:* see Note 48. An American version, *The Crucifixion, by an Eye-Witness*, was published in Chicago in 1907 by the Indo-American Company. It is probable that it had contacts with India, as indicated by its name. This version is still being reprinted in Pakistan, and it was translated into Urdu at an early date. In the 1890s, Ahmad already showed interest in theories that Jesus had survived the crucifixion and he promoted an oil, which he said had been used for curing Jesus, and which he claimed to be effective against the bubonic plague. *The Essene Letter* is used as a source in several Ahmadiyya books, such as in J. D. Shams, *Where did Jesus Die?*, 7th ed. (London: Shams Brothers, 1978); Mohammad Yasin, *Rauzabal and other Mysteries of Kashmir* (Srinagar: Kesar Publications, 1972), pp. 3–5, 9; Aziz Kashmiri, *Christ in Kashmir* (Srinagar: Roshni Publications, 1973), pp. 15–18.

79. *Notovitch:* See Ahmad, *Jesus in India*, p. 122. Ahmad quotes here the beginning of Max Müller's critical article in *The Nineteenth Century*, 1894, but breaks off the quotation before the devastating criticism. It is possible that Ahmad did not commit conscious fraud but had difficulty in understanding the English article; Müller is misquoted in a way that may indicate this. Ahmad's disciples have also been using Notovitch: Shams' book contains extracts from *The Life of St. Issa;* cf. Yasin, p. 10. Kashmiri, p. 56, quotes Max Müller's article, also omitting the criticism. In an interview Mirza Nasir Ahmad, the present caliph for Ahmad, mentions Notovitch's "discovery" without indicating his name or Hemis. According to his view, there are about ten (!) books in the monastery that mention the Messiah (interview in the Swedish magazine *Sökaren* 1978:8). A contrary legend, spread in Scandinavia at present, says that the manuscript was stolen from the monastery by a Muslim doctor, named Ahmad Shah,

at the instigation of "the British Church in India"; thus the matter seems quite open to the play of anyone's imagination. Faber-Kaiser has a totally uncritical account of Notovitch's story in *Jesus in Kashmir,* pp. 10–20.

80. *Hassnain:* According to reports in the Swedish press. *Kashmiri: Christ in Kashmir,* pl. 13.

81. *Jesus in Japan:* The report is taken from an article by Michael Hornby, "Did Jesus die aged 106 in Japan?," *The Times* (London), 28 December 1970.

82. *The Q Document:* See Note 8 above.

83. The complete title is *The Gospel of the Holy Twelve: known also as the Gospel of the Perfect Life, translated from the Aramaic and edited by a disciple of the Master, and with former editions compared and revised,* Issued by the Order of At-one-ment and United Templars' Society, Paris, Jerusalem, Madras. The first edition has no indication of place and year, but was probably printed in Brighton, England, in 1901. The second edition is unknown, but the third edition was printed in Brighton in 1903. What the "former editions" were cannot be established; it is possible that they were handwritten copies. The text was reprinted in E. F. Udny, *The Original Christianity in the Gospel of the Holy Twelve* (London: Edson Ltd., 1924). The original edition as well as Udny's reprint are difficult to find today; the copies at the British Library were destroyed during World War II. There are, however, some later editions, which have the same title as the original edition and probably the same text. One has been published by John M. Watkins, London 1957, and has a preface written by Ronald Hentland, a relative of Anna Kingsford (see Note 93 below). Hentland says that he obtained permission for this edition from S. H. Hart, who owned the manuscript, and who published the third edition of Anna Kingsford's biography. The latest edition that I know of was published by The Christian Gospel Trust, Henley Bridge House, Ashburnham, Battle, Sussex, 1972. This is said to be the seventh edition, but I know of only five editions before this latest one. (I have probably missed one.) Both these later editions (and probably the earlier ones) also contain *The Epistle of Appollos the Prophet to Hierasthenes.* I have not studied this apocryphon very closely.

84. *Abba-Amma:* I presume that this is the same (kabbalistic) Father-Mother principle that Madame Blavatsky names Abba Amona in her *Theosophical Glossary* (London 1892), p. 2.

85. *The shortest and the most difficult reading:* The technical terms are *lectio brevior* and *lectio difficilior.* It is more common that a copyist will add words rather than subtract them, and it is also more likely that he will clarify a difficult passage than make a clear statement more obscure.

86. *The apocryphal Jesus saying* belonged to the now lost *Gospel of the Egyptians,* and is quoted in the so-called *Second Epistle of Clement* 12:2, in *The Acts of Peter* 38 and in *The Acts of Philip* 146. It also appears in *The Gospel of Thomas* as logion (saying) 23.

87. *Trinity:* The earliest evidence for the word is found in Theophilus of Antioch, *To Autolycus* 2.15, and in a fragment of a writing by the Gnostic Theodorus. Both are from the second century.

88. *Filioque:* The earliest evidence for the insertion of this word into the Nicene Creed is from a synod in Fréjus in southern France in 796. See Jaroslav Pelikan, *The Christian Tradition*, vol. 2 (Chicago: University of Chicago Press, 1974), p. 184.

89. *The wedding ceremony:* The custom of holding crowns or wreaths over bride and bridegroom, as well as the "dance" performed by the bridal couple and the priest around the altar, are well-known elements in the Orthodox marriage ritual even today. Crowning the bridal couple was originally a pagan custom, which was subsequently accepted by Christians. See Karl Baus, *Der Kranz in Antike und Christentum* (= Theophaneia 2) Bonn 1940, pp. 98–111.

90. *The Commixtio:* After the consecration in the Roman Mass, the priest lays a piece of the host in the chalice with a prayer for the sanctification of this holy union of the Body and Blood of Christ. The custom originated in the papal Mass in the early Middle Ages.

91. *Ouseley's life and work:* Some of the information here comes from the 1972 edition of *The Gospel of the Holy Twelve.* Most of it, however, comes from the Brighton Public Library, which gathered the information because Ouseley gave a copy of the third edition of his book to the library in 1903. This information was transmitted to me by a Norwegian minister, the Rev. J. Huseklepp, and two others.

92. *Ouseley's writings:* See the *British Museum General Catalogue* under the entry Ouseley, Gideon Jasper Richard. The list, however, is not quite complete. A booklet entitled *The Church of the Future* is listed in *The National Union Catalogue*, Pre-1956 Imprints, vol. 435, p. 356 and vol. 432, p. 8. *The Clerical Directory* of 1882 lists ten more titles; these books, however, have never been traced. The titles of the books mention various unknown organizations, such as The Order of the At-one-ment, United Templars' Society, and The Order of the Golden Age. The last-mentioned order is said to have been founded in 1895 to hasten the arrival of a coming golden age by a vegetarian diet. The two other organizations are completely unknown to me as well as to the Brighton Public Library. According to the preface of Ouseley's Gospel, The Order of the At-one-ment was founded in 1881.

93. *Kingsford and Maitland:* Anna Bonus Kingsford (1846–1888) was the wife of an English clergyman. Her interest in antivivisectionism led her to leave England for medical studies in Paris. She was accompanied by Edward Maitland – her husband remained at home in his parish – and the two began a curious career together. Anna soon revealed prophetic gifts, and her prophecies contained a mixture of Christian and pagan Greek beliefs. Maitland and Kingsford founded together a "Hermetic Society" with a kind of theosophical ideology as its basis. The circle of those in-

terested is said to have included Lady Wilde and her two sons, Oscar and William. After Anna's premature death, Edward Maitland published her biography, *Anna Kingsford, Her life, letters, diary and work*, vols. 1 and 2 (London 1896), the only comprehensive work there is about her. A third edition was published by S. H. Hart in 1913 (also see the following note). Kingsford's and Maitland's "hermetism" was soon superseded by Madame Blavatsky's more successful branch of theosophy.

94. *"I. O.":* Maitland, 1st ed., p. 76. Ouseley published several books under the pseudonym "I. O." See the *British Museum General Catalogue* under Ouseley, Gideon Jasper Richard. The connection between Ouseley and the couple Kingsford-Maitland is confirmed by the fact that the manuscript of his "Gospel" became the property of S. H. Hart (according to the preface of the 1957 edition). As we have seen, Hart was the editor of the third edition of Maitland's biography of Anna Kingsford. The preface of the 1957 edition of the "Gospel" was written by a relative of Anna Kingsford.

95. *Swedenborg's revelation about Maitland:* See S. H. Hart's preface to his edition of Anna Kingsford's biography.

96. *The preface of the "Gospel"* is worth quoting *in extenso:* "Their 'Gospel of the Holy Twelve' was communicated to the Editors, in numerous fragments at different times, by Emmanuel Swedenborg, Anna Kingsford, Edward Maitland, and a priest of a former century, giving his name as Placidus, of the Franciscan Order. By them it was translated from the original, and given to the Editors in the flesh, to be supplemented in their proper places, where indicated, from the 'four Gospels' (A. V.) as revised by the same" (from the third edition, according to a copy made by Brighton Public Library).

97. *Annie Besant:* In *The Theosophical Review*, 1902, p. 572 f.

98. *The Aquarian Gospel of Jesus the Christ:* The first edition was published in Los Angeles in 1911. I have used a paperback edition from 1972, published by DeVorss & Company, Marina del Rey, California. It is probably still being reprinted; I have seen a copy of the fourth reprint from 1976. The English edition is published by L. N. Fouler & Son. I have seen the 24th reprint from 1977.

99. *Matheno and Meng-ste:* Noted by Goodspeed. *Kaspar:* As a name for one of the Magi, *Kaspar* first appears in a work by the historian Agnellus (ninth century). In an earlier manuscript he is called Gathaspa; it probably refers to the Parthian king Gundafurr, who is a personage in the ancient *Acts of Thomas*, but who belongs to the first century B.C. See Ugo Monneret de Villard, *Le leggende orientali sui magi evangelici* (= Studi e Testi 163), Città del Vaticano 1952, p. 25.

100. *Levi H. Dowling:* Biographical information is found in the paperback edition of *The Aquarian Gospel*, 1972. See also Goodspeed, p. 15 ff.

101. *The Ancient Catholic Church:* Peter F. Anson, *Bishops at Large. Nicholas Roerich:* See above, note 75. (London: Faber & Faber, 1964),

p. 474 f.

102. *Apulcius:* See Robert Graves, *Apuleius' The Golden Ass* (New York: Farrar, Straus and Giroux, 1951).

103. *The Magus:* See Eliza Butler, *The Myth of the Magus* (New York: MacMillan Co., 1948).

104. *Christian Rosencreutz:* The most important document is the *Fama Fraternitatis* from 1615. A good English translation is found in Frances A. Yates, *The Rosicrucian Enlightenment* (London and Boston: Routledge & Kegan Paul, 1972), pp. 238–242. The ideological background of the book is treated on p. 43. Some important corrections to Yates' account are found in John Warwick Montgomery, *Cross and Crucible*, 1–2 (Nijhoff: The Hague, 1973).

105. *Saint-Germain:* See Christopher McIntosh, *Eliphas Levi and the French Occult Revival* (London: Rider, 1972), p. 18, where the count is connected with Apollonius and Christian Rosencreutz. What he really did during his obscure career is uncertain.

106. *The Gospel of Peace:* The first edition is *The Gospel of Peace of Jesus Christ by the disciple John,* Aramaic and Old Slavonic Texts compared and ed. by Edmond Szekely and Purcell Weaver (Ashingdon, Rochford, Essex: C. W. Daniel Company Limited and Leatherhead, Surrey: Bureau of Cosmotherapy, Lawrence Weaver House, 1937). In this form and with this title, the book has been reprinted many times, and is probably still being reprinted by the C. W. Daniel Company, now in London. I have seen an unchanged reprint from 1977. The continuation is published in England as *The Gospel of the Essenes* in one volume by the same publisher. The American edition has the title *The Essene Gospel of Peace,* and was published by the International Biogenic Society, Cartago, Costa Rica, probably an affiliation of the same institute in San Diego, where Szekely lived. The first volume, printed in 1978, has the subtitle *The Third Century Aramaic Manuscript and Old Slavonic Texts Compared, Edited, and Translated by Edmond Bordeaux Szekely.* Its content is identical with the original *Gospel of Peace,* but the preface has been considerably altered. The two other volumes, printed in 1977 and 1978 respectively, are subtitled *The Unknown Books of the Essenes* and *Lost Scrolls of the Essene Brotherhood* Both are said to have been translated by Szekely from Hebrew and Aramaic original texts. Their content corresponds to the English *Gospel of the Essenes.*

107. *Szekely's youth* has been described by himself in *The Discovery of the Essene Gospel of Peace,* (San Diego: Academy Books, 1977). I have supplemented his statements there with information from the catalogue of The International Biogenic Institute, which seems to list most of his many books. Szekely later dropped the accent over the first e in his name; I generally leave it out.

108. *Szekely's ancestors:* See Constantin von Wurzbach, *Biographisches Lexikon des Kaiserthums Oesterreichs,* vol. 42 (Vienna, n.d.) p. 13 f., and

vol. 3 (Vienna 1858), pp. 65–69.

109. *The Secret Archives:* See *The Discovery,* p. 50. Szekely's description of the archives as an immense labyrinth of unsorted manuscripts seems romantically overstated, even if it does describe its condition fifty years ago.

110. *The account of the discovery* appears in a most astonishing way, namely as a side issue to the find of the Hebrew Monte Cassino fragments: "I had found the Source: Hebrew fragments of the Essene Gospel, the Aramaic version of which I had just read (!) from the shelves of Msgr. Mercati's locked room" (*The Discovery,* p. 54). This is positively all that is said about the Aramaic text, which is the basis of the edition of *The Gospel of Peace!*

111. *Szekely in Paris: The Discovery,* p. 45.

112. *Szekely and Huxley: The Essene Gospel of Peace,* vol. 2, preface, p. 9.

113. *The Old Slavonic manuscript:* Also see the subtitle of the 1937 edition, where the translation is said to be based on a comparison between Aramaic and Old Slavonic texts. Zimmerman's account of the date of its discovery appears in the introduction to his German translation of *The Gospel of Peace* (vol. 1), which he has given the more teutonic-sounding title *Heliand.* I have used the third edition, published by Eduard Fankhauser Verlag, Thielle/Neuch. 1956; it is printed in one volume with the *Evangelium des vollkommenen Lebens,* Zimmermann's abbreviated translation of *The Gospel of the Holy Twelve.* Szekely's own account of the route is found in *The Discovery,* p. 37.

114. *The Hebrew text:* My linguistic expert is Mr. Bo Lundén, M. A., Lund. His general impression is that the text is fairly late but with some archaisms and expressions from biblical Hebrew. There is nothing against the theory that it might have been written in our own time.

115. *Zimmermann's visit to Szekely:* The account appears in a footnote in the 1956 edition of *Heliand,* p. 6.

116. *The original preface:* See the original edition from 1937, p. 5: "His words became half forgotten and were not collected till some generations after they were uttered. They have been misunderstood, wrongly annotated, hundreds of times rewritten and hundreds of times transformed, yet they have nevertheless survived almost two thousand years . . . It is a heavy responsibility to proclaim the present New Testament, which is the basis of all the Christian Churches, as deformed and falsified, but there is no higher religion than the truth."

117. *Saint John as author:* In the American edition, John is omitted from .he title of the first volume, but he appears in vol. 2, p. 97, this time as the author of a short paraphrase of some passages from the Fourth Gospel.

118. *Weaver:* For his books, see the *British Museum General Catalogue,* under Weaver, Lawrence Purcell. To be fair, I should mention that he is also a linguist, and is now teaching Latin at the University of Santa Barbara, California As far as I know, however, he has no knowledge of

Notes

Aramaic or Old Slavonic.

119. *The inaccessible manuscripts:* One of the many riddles is where the Vienna manuscript is now. According to *Heliand,* 1956 edition, p. 3 f., Szekely told Zimmermann that the manuscript was no longer in Vienna but had become the property of the Vatican library. But in the latest American edition, in the same preface where Szekely has made so many changes, the statement that the Old Slavonic manuscript is in Vienna remains unaltered.

120. *The Vienna manuscript:* According to a letter to me from Dr. Eva Irblich of the manuscript and incunabula division of the Austrian National Library, dated 3 October 1979. Cf. Gerhard Birkfellner, *Glagolitische und kyrillische Handschriften in Österreich,* Vienna 1975.

121. *The letter from Msgr. Giusti* is dated 12 June 1978. I here quote it *in extenso:* "Dear Sir, Thank you for your letter of 25th May inquiring about Edmond Bordeaux Székely. This author's book is known to me and I can assert categorically that no such manuscript of an Aramaic Gospel is possessed by the Vatican Archives. Moreover, Székely's name has not been found in the card index of scholars admitted to the Archives and I know of no reason why the name of Monsignor Mercati should be associated with his. With every good wish, Yours sincerely, (signature) Msgr. Martino Giusti Prefect."

122. The quotation is from *The Essene Gospel of Peace,* vol. 1, p. 22 f.

123. The quotation has been taken from p. 17 f.

124. *The Jesus Scroll* was published by Angus & Robertson in 1973; a paperback edition from Sphere Books followed in 1975.

125. *Masada:* See Yigael Yadin, *Masada, Herod's Fortress and the Zealots' Last Stand* (New York: Random House, 1966).

126. The quotation from *The Jesus Scroll* is from the paperback edition, p. 170 f.

127. *The Secret Gospel of Mark:* See Morton Smith, *Clement of Alexandria and a Secret Gospel of Mark* (Cambridge: Harvard University Press, 1973). *Idem, The Secret Gospel: The Discovery and Interpretation of the Secret Gospel According to Mark* (New York: Harper & Row, 1973).

128. *Photographs of the manuscript: Clement of Alexandria,* plates on pp. 449–453. *The Secret Gospel,* p. 39, contains a photograph of the printed book from 1646 with the first page of the manuscript.

129. *The authenticity of the letter of Clement:* Opinion about this is not unanimous. Among those who have denied the authenticity of the letter are prominent scholars such as Arthur Darby Nock, Johannes Munck, and Wilhelm Völker. See *Clement of Alexandria,* p. 67 and 88, note 1: *The Secret Gospel,* p. 27 ff. Paul J. Achtemeier adopts a waiting policy in his review in the *Journal of Biblical Literature,* no. 93 (1974), pp. 625–628. "R. P. C. Hanson" is bound to accept the document as genuine but is very critical about Smith's use of it, *The Journal of Theological Studies,* no. 25 (1974), pp. 513–521. F. F. Bruce considers the Gospel frag-

ment to be a forgery but the letter of Clement to be genuine and thinks that Clement has quoted a circulating Gospel pastiche, *The "Secret" Gospel of Mark*, Ethel Wood Lecture, 11 February 1974 (London: The Athlone Press, 1974).

130. *Parallels in the fourth gospel* have been noted by Walter Wink in *Union Seminary Quarterly Review*, no. 30 (1974), pp. 3–14. It is a most remarkable review, for after a number of very grave objections against Smith's method it ends with almost lyrical praise of Smith for the tremendous achievement he is said to have made by his new image of Jesus.

131. *Clement index:* By Otto Stählin in *Griechische Christliche Schriftsteller* 39.1–2, Berlin 1934–36.

132. *Did Jesus baptize?* There is a faint allusion in John 4:1 f.

133. *St. Mark in Alexandria:* Eusebius' account stands in his *Ecclesiastical History* II.16. See A. Böhlig, art. Aegypten, *Reallexikon für Antike und Christentum*, 1 (1950), col. 131.

134. *Quentin Quesnell,* "The Mar Saba Clementine: A Question of Evidence," *The Catholic Biblical Quarterly,* vol. 37 (1975), pp. 48–67. He here quotes Goodspeed's earlier version of his book, *Strange New Gospels*, 1931. *The lack of photographs:* In his answer to Quesnell (see below), Morton Smith makes the Harvard University Press responsible, but does not promise better photographs. The photograph in *The Secret Gospel* has the margins clearly visible, but this is only one page of the manuscript. *Morton Smith's counterattack,* "On the Authenticity of the Mar Saba Letter of Clement," *The Catholic Biblical Quarterly,* vol. 38 (1976), pp. 196–199, is followed by Quentin Quesnell, "A Reply to Morton Smith," in the same issue, pp. 200–203.

135. *Morton Smith's theses:* See Quesnell, "The Mar Saba Clementine," p. 59. Smith's objections and his claim to have been misquoted do not seem quite convincing. Morton Smith has presented his view of Jesus in a monograph, *Jesus the Magician* (San Francisco: Harper & Row, 1978; English edition, London: Gollancz, 1978). *The Secret Gospel of Mark* is mentioned sometimes, and is even given the honorific title of "the longer Marcan text" (American edition, p. 134 and footnote, p. 207). More striking is that it has very little importance for Smith's argumentation in general. He seems to have formed his view of Jesus quite independently of his find. As far as I can see, the alleged homosexuality is not mentioned this time.

136. The letter quoted is from Mr. Richard Matz, Swedish translator of Martin Heidegger's works. English translation by me.

Index of Names

Index of Titles

Index of Titles